MW00714528

Presented To:

_____

From:

_____

Date:

_____

Everyday Wisdom

by
James S. Bell Jr.
and
Stan Campbell

RIVER
OAK
PUBLISHING

Everyday Wisdom
ISBN 1-58919-791-7
Copyright 2001 © by RiverOak Publishing
P.O. Box 700143
Tulsa, Oklahoma 74170-0143

To my father, who told me years ago
that you had to be both street smart
and intelligent to make a difference.
And to my mother, who told me
to use both human and divine
methods to get the job done.

—James S. Bell Jr.

INTRODUCTION

Many books on the shelves today, especially in the business section, tell you how to be "street smart," that is, how to deal with others in a shrewd and cunning way in order to get ahead in life. If you look in the religion or self-help sections, you'll learn how to be "pure of heart," which means being humble, perfect in your motives, putting others first. The problem is, most of us want both. We want to survive and come out on top, but we want to do it ethically, both helping and respecting others in the process.

This conundrum isn't new. Philosophers and business people alike have attempted to construct methods of combining these two principles in their work and life practices. Similar to the principles discussed in *A Return to Virtue,* the other book we coauthored, this book presents some thoughts about how to succeed and to do so morally. Our commentaries seek to provide a friendly guide to show you how to use opportunities to your own advantage and make both you and what you accomplish a benefit and blessing to others.

Many of the thoughts expressed here were written for those trying to find their place in the world, learning how to get along with others to attain personal and professional growth. This is largely connected with the virtues of wisdom and prudence. Prudence, especially, is misunderstood today. It is the quality of being cautious, balanced, moderate, and calculating in everything. It is a key to avoid being sidetracked from your goals.

We are firm believers that human effort isn't sufficient without the time-honored values of faith and morals. At the same time, the greatest code of ethics will not take the place of being diligent and shrewd. A fifteenth-century Jesuit priest and respected thinker, Baltasar Gracian, offers a fitting analogy illustrating this point. He contrasts the serpent and the dove and suggests taking on attributes of each, as both craftiness and innocence are needed when dealing with others. The shrewdness of a serpent provides self-protection and helps assess strengths, weaknesses, and motives. The innocence of a dove prevents one from being overly suspicious or judgmental as he or she seeks to serve others.

Whatever your circumstances, it is our hope that this volume will make you a closer friend of the wise.

—James S. Bell Jr. and Stan Campbell

A ONCE-IN-A-LIFETIME TRIP

Use wisdom as you set goals for your life. Don't let chance govern your steps, but use foresight and have a sense of balance. Include some pleasures; grow in knowledge that may increase your enjoyment. But you will not always find beauty in beautiful places; our heavenly Father distributes blessing in plain appearance as well.

Suppose a hard-working New Yorker gets a well-deserved three-week vacation and decides he wants to "see America." He might approach his time off in a couple of ways. His first option is to get into his car and head for the sunset with no plans, no maps, and no schedule. He can drive for ten days or hit the Pacific Ocean, whichever comes first, and then turn around and start home. There he can tell friends about seeing fields, trees, mountains, and such.

Or he can start out with maps and an itinerary. He can drive with specific destinations in mind: the Grand Canyon, Yellowstone, Yosemite, or the Golden Gate bridge. He will still see fields, trees, and mountains, but the slide show of his trip is likely to be considerably more interesting.

Of course, if he takes a trip like this every year, he has the freedom to occasionally wander aimlessly. But if it's a once-in-a-lifetime trip, he will want to make the most of it.

A person's life is a once-in-a-lifetime trip. Sometimes it seems we have all the time in the world, but we don't. To live effectively, we must set goals and accumulate some memorable achievements. While we certainly want to plan periods of time for leisurely sightseeing, we cannot afford to miss out on the things of importance— whatever we determine those things to be.

Use foresight. Have a sense of balance. You won't get another chance.

CONSEQUENCES AND TRUTH

Communicate nothing but truth, yet don't divulge everything. It takes good character both to reveal as well as to conceal truth. One lie can ruin your entire reputation. Deceit is often put on the level of treason, which in turn makes you a traitor. Yet you need not tell everything—to your benefit and the benefit of others.

In a courtroom you might be called on to provide "the truth, the whole truth, and nothing but the truth." But in casual, day-to-day relationships with those around us, it may sometimes be wise to avoid "the whole truth."

This is a nice greeting: "Good morning, Mrs. Johnson. It's a lovely day, isn't it?" You might even want to add a truthful observation: "That's a beautiful sweater!" But now suppose you add another honest opinion: "Too bad your hat looks as if your cats have been hacking up hairballs all over it." You've just stepped over the line in divulging truth. At issue is your character, not the truthfulness of your statement.

Your evaluation might be 100 percent true. Everyone else on the block might agree with you. But there is no need to bludgeon poor Mrs. Johnson with that bit of truth. In this case (and in thousands of similar instances), a portion of the truth is best kept to yourself.

You probably know people who, whenever a rare thought drifts through their minds, feel obliged to share it with the world, regardless of its relevance. Others try so hard to impress people that their thoughts quickly evolve into exaggerations, then outright lies, and perhaps even full-fledged deceit. No one likes to be around such people.

We must begin today to practice telling the truth, the relevant truth, and no bit of truth that does unnecessary harm.

AN "E" FOR EXCELLENCE

Strive for excellence in tasks judged to be excellent. Those who are great succeed in what is considered to be most worthwhile. Average performance never wins recognition. Excellence is the noblest characteristic—it generates admiration and favor.

Why is it that people pay hundreds of dollars to attend business seminars when they could read a fifteen-dollar book to glean similar information? Why do we try to get out of going to a niece's fifth-grade concert, yet eagerly seek tickets to the Chicago Symphony or to hear the Beach Boys? Why do some of the most apathetic sports fans get caught up in "Super Bowl fever" or collegiate basketball "March Madness"?

One reason is we tend to be fascinated by those who are at the top of their fields. It might be music, business, sports, or any other category. You might care little for figure skating or track and field, for instance, yet find yourself absorbed by Olympic athletes who have mastered the skills involved.

Why is this? Perhaps we know at the deepest levels of ourselves what was required for the person to get to the top. Hard decisions had to be made. Sacrifices of time and energy were required. Many worthwhile pursuits had to be abandoned in order to excel in one particular area.

Sometimes we are too quick to grade ourselves with a big "E" for effort. In certain instances we deserve to do so. But if we aren't also earning some "E's" for excellence in other areas, perhaps we are letting ourselves off too easily. You may never pitch a World Series game or dance the lead in *Swan Lake,* but you do have opportunities—if you are willing to define and pursue them—to excel at something.

When you succeed in what is considered to be most worthwhile, people will notice. And the satisfaction you feel will be excellent!

TONGUE DEPRESSORS

Don't be involved in gossip. If you are taken for that sort of person, you might also be suspected of slandering others' reputations. Avoid using your wit at the expense of your neighbors. They will eventually pay you back by ganging up on you—the word of the many against the one.

Suppose Joe, the office gossip, walks up to you and says: "Hey, did you hear about Ray? His wife was out of town last night—supposedly visiting her family. I hear their marriage isn't working out so well. And his secretary—you know Sue, don't you? The young blond with the "woo-woo" figure? Anyway, she was supposed to drop off some papers at his house last night. From what I hear, she was there quite awhile." Then, with a wink and a knowing look, he walks away.

How do you suppose you will feel if you unexpectedly run into Ray or Sue during the day? If Sue discovers that Joe has been talking about her, how will she feel about your being a participant? And even worse, how will you feel the next time you see Joe talking to a coworker, glancing in your direction? Will he be talking about you?

Being privy to gossip is a no-win situation. You can't believe all, if any, of what you've heard. And as soon as you open your ears to gossip, you open your reputation to question. Even as an unwilling party to the latest news on the grapevine, you are labeled as a certain kind of person.

How much better it is to be someone whom people can trust to be discreet with their honest and open feelings. Vulnerability and intimacy cannot exist in the Land of Gossip. It seems harmless and painless to shoot off your mouth occasionally. But the distance is never long between being the "shooter" and becoming the target for someone else's verbal arrows. When you're the target, you discover the harm and the pain that are involved. You also see that you are one person against the many who eventually pay you back by ganging up on you.

So whenever you choose gossip over truth and integrity, you may as well get ready. Your time is coming.

THE SKY MAY (OR MAY NOT) BE FALLING

Be careful with the information you receive. We thrive on facts rather than what is merely visible on the surface. The truth rarely comes in pure form but is affected by the moods and purposes of the messenger. So be alert to the intentions of the source. Be aware ahead of time of his or her purpose. Test for false elements or exaggeration.

When Chicken Little got bonked on the head with an acorn, she immediately became vehement in her mission to spread the news that, "The sky is falling." No one could question the hen's intentions or intensity, but she simply didn't have her facts straight.

We all communicate feelings as well as facts. And when the facts and feelings are tightly entwined, it becomes quite difficult for the listener to discern between them. We may not even notice when we do it, so it's an even greater challenge to detect when someone else does. Yet it is quite unwise to take everything we hear—even from a firsthand source— at face value.

Recent studies have been conducted to see to what extent eyewitness testimony can be trusted. Many of the results are alarming. In the heat of the moment and the ensuing panic after a hit-and-run accident, bank robbery, or drive-by shooting, witnesses don't remember nearly as well as they think they do. In many cases, people are ready to convict the wrong person just because of the color of his shirt or the style of her hair.

We need to be more accurate in our presentation of facts. And just as importantly, we need to be discerning when listening to other people. If we're not careful, we can be grossly misled by someone else's pending divorce, resentment toward the boss, indigestion, or any number of other factors.

Don't just use your ears when receiving information. Use your head as well. Remember Chicken Little. The sky may not be falling. It may simply be one more nut on the loose.

DON'T SMILE: YOU'RE ON CANDID CAMERA!

Always think and behave as if others were watching you. Walls have ears, as the saying goes, and bad deeds will come back to haunt you. Even if you are alone, act as if the eyes of the whole world are upon you. Consider these imaginary people as witnesses who would have heard of your actions at a later time anyway. Live as if you don't mind your neighbors looking in the windows.

Suppose you discover that someone has recorded your every move, both public and private, for the past month. If he threatened a public viewing, inviting everyone involved, would you be eager to recover the tape before he could do so? What would you be willing to pay to prevent public exposure?

These days it seems that no revealed secret is too shocking for some people. Just click your remote control through daytime TV talk shows and see what people are sharing about themselves to millions of viewers at a time. For them, such videotape of their "indiscretions" would only make them more marketable. Yet others might pay large sums of money to prevent their indiscretions from becoming public.

In the early days of TV, a program called *Candid Camera* was popular because the producers would set up humorous and slightly embarrassing situations to try and catch people when they weren't at their best. The goal was to get the person to smile when he discovered his actions were being observed. These days, however, the exploits of *Candid Camera* would be far too tame.

What would be rare and unique is the discovery of someone with nothing to be ashamed of and little, if anything, to be embarrassed by. These people would never make it to TV, though, because nobody wants to watch someone setting a good example and behaving respectably. In fact, if you want people watching your every move, all you need to do is misbehave—they'll flock to you. But if you want their eager eyes to keep wandering, don't give them anything to look at. They'll soon be on their way to look for someone a lot more interesting. And you can keep looking out for yourself.

THE WEIGHT OF THE WAIT

Never let problems come to a boiling point. Your reputation will always suffer. Hidden enemies may wait in ambush for this possibility. Even friends may cover their own mistakes by hiding behind your faults. Under such circumstances, it is difficult to be either patient or wise.

Have you ever considered what percentage of your problems are situations you could deal with and put behind you if you only would? For example, do any of these things apply to you?

> Do you cringe every time the phone rings, hoping it isn't a particular person you aren't ready to talk to?
>
> Are you and a neighbor at odds about a minor incident?
>
> Have you and a family member exchanged harsh words, both waiting for the other to be the first to reconcile?
>
> Do you know of anyone at work who has something against you?

Are you content with your physical condition:
exercise, diet, etc.?

All of these are areas of life which you have the
power to do something about. If you choose not to, they
can add up to quite a lot of stress. If left unattended for
long enough, they can reach a "boiling point." Minor
incidents can become lawsuits. Harsh words can cause
rebellion. Lack of physical exercise leads to numerous
health problems.

Life throws us enough things we can't control, so
street-smart people will become proactive in the things
they can. A phone call here, a note of apology there,
and a few other minor actions can do much to smooth out
potential rough spots in life. The alternative is risking
personal reputation, relationships, good health, and peace
of mind. Friends will slink away, and enemies will gloat.

The next time you're feeling the heat, seek a "cooling
point" rather than a boiling point. Like a fresh-baked
pie placed on a windowsill to cool, your relationships
will be strongest if you don't let them get too hot or too
cold. It can be a challenge to keep them all warm and
friendly, but it's worth the effort.

ONE PEACE AT A TIME

A peaceful life leads to long life. Peacemakers will not merely survive; they will be in control of their lives. A day without an argument brings peaceful sleep. It is folly to worry about what does not concern you or to take everything personally.

It may be hard for some people to think about the concept of peace without recalling the hippie movement of the 1960s. Despite what you might think of hippie politics or lifestyle choices, the desire for peace was a noble sentiment. Their pursuit of peace, on the other hand, was perhaps a bit naive and shortsighted.

The hippies eventually discovered that peace is not an isolated experience. Peace must have a context. It's not enough to retire to a remote commune in the country, leaving the world behind and greeting one another with two fingers in a V and a salutation of, "Peace, man." Such "peace" has little, if any, benefit.

We discover the true value of peace in the context of a hectic workplace, a troubled family situation, or a life-threatening disease. In fact, any tense situation is where peace is needed most. It is under these circumstances where it is most important to act in a spirit of peace. We can let these conditions control us, or we can choose to control them. We need not add to our misery by holding grudges, arguing about minute disagreements, or demanding our way in every little issue. We might win every time, but it won't be a peaceful experience.

Let your thin skin thicken a little. Don't be so quick to fight someone else's battles. Steal a moment of peace wherever you can find it. As you get better at this peace-by-peace approach to life, you'll soon discover you're coping with life better than you ever expected. And when you go to bed at night: sweet dreams.

RIPE BUT NOT ROTTEN

Try to reach your peak of perfection and realize you are not born that way. We develop our personal gifts in our professions one day at a time. They are realized by discriminating taste, precise thinking, mature judgment, and a determined will. Some never reach completeness in these areas, whereas others ripen late.

The goal of maturity is to look forward and get a little better and wiser each day. But the way we evaluate our maturing process is by looking backward. Think of yourself a year ago, five years ago, ten years ago. While perhaps you can be proud of your accomplishments, you are likely to see a much more immature person. You might even be a bit embarrassed to think of how you used to act and respond in certain situations compared to how you react now.

A grapefruit hanging on a tree will ripen through a gradual process. It doesn't take long for the fruit to look ripe, but in actuality it may still be quite sour. Yet in time, the inner portion will sweeten and mature to the point that it matches the appearance of its outer demeanor.

People are much the same. We mature year by year. In a few instances we may reach a peak of perfection, where we become leaders in a particular field of expertise. In such cases, after the maturing process has essentially been completed, the goal is to keep from becoming rotten.

We have much to learn from experts, and we have much to teach others in our field. Yet no one likes to be around an accomplished expert who knows it and shows it. The sweetness of expertise disappears in the presence of the stench of pride and self-satisfaction.

Others will flock to you if you are ripe and appealing. They will forgive you if you're a bit green but continuing to ripen day by day. But if you reach the top and then lose the humility that got you there, don't be surprised to be treated like any other rotten piece of fruit that's past its prime.

THE TRUTH LIES SOMEWHERE

Never exaggerate. Remember not to make good things seem better, or you will stretch the truth and cast doubt on your own judgment. A wise person prefers to underestimate the value of something. Extraordinary things are rare, so modify your evaluations and keep your reputation.

A judge made national headlines because of his dishonesty. He hadn't fixed any trials. He didn't take any bribes. But he did tell friends and peers that he had received the Congressional Medal of Honor—a seemingly harmless lie. Yet when others discovered his willingness to stretch the truth, they quickly cast doubt on his judgment. His harmless lie destroyed his otherwise good reputation.

It's amazing we don't hear thousands of similar stories. After all, we are bombarded with gross exaggerations and senseless superlatives every day in the form of advertising: highest in protein, lowest in price, longest lasting, maximum strength, quickest to act, safest to use, best in its class. Consequently, wise consumers tend to cast doubt on such claims.

But advertisers aren't the only culprits. Anyone perusing a random sampling of résumés from recent graduates might think he or she had stumbled onto the dossiers of Mensa members or Nobel Prize winners. Experience is exaggerated to the point that anyone who can work a TV remote seems eager to claim "skill at operating advanced electronic equipment." How can a potential employer make wise judgments when the exaggeration syndrome is so widespread?

Honorable people have no need to exaggerate. They need only make a statement and then stand by it. Of course, in the present day and age, no one will believe you—not at first. But with consistency, people will eventually learn that you say what you mean and mean what you say. They will be surprised to have discovered a rarity in today's world—a person of honor. And you won't need a medal to prove it.

THE PRICE OF PEACE

Don't take on the innocence of a dove to an extreme. Alternate this quality with the cunning of a serpent. Some are not deceived through foolishness—but through sheer goodness that trusts to a fault. Two kinds of people protect themselves from harm: those who have suffered directly and those who observe others who pay the price.

A proven strategy for creating likable characters in Hollywood seems to be to start with someone who appears ordinary—or even below average—and then bestow the person with skills and abilities of which no one is aware. Clark Kent's mild manner shrouds his super strength. Lowly Mr. Miyagi of *The Karate Kid* is the last person someone would expect to be a black belt. And beneath Columbo's rumpled raincoat and awkwardness is a razor-sharp mind that solves every case.

Perhaps these characters are so popular because we envy their ability to maintain mild-mannered and peaceful lives. Such peace can rarely, if ever, exist without exercising other inner strengths on occasion. As hard as we try to live as innocently as doves, not everyone is going to respect our wishes. Even nesting songbirds know that when a hawk threatens them, they must boldly chase away the larger bird. What they lack in size and power, they make up for in determination.

Peace is seldom possible without power to accomplish and defend it. The freedom of the United States required a revolution. We have civil rights due to past and present struggles. Any level of personal peace and freedom will require a strong stand against those who threaten us. We owe others the benefit of the doubt. Yet, if they deceive us time after time, our doubts become confirmed, and we should change strategies.

As you deal with others, remember that blessed are the peacemakers. But when peacemaking doesn't work, blessed are those who do what is right—regardless of the cost.

NOW WOULD BE GOOD

The wise do at once what fools do too late. Both may do the same thing, but the difference is timing. The one who begins with his thinking upside down will continue in the same approach to the end. You must force the fool in the right direction. But the wise man acts quickly and willingly to his gain.

It used to be that people could procrastinate and then make an art out of getting away with it by using creative excuses. Yet the onset of the information age is bringing accountability to those with the "better late than never" philosophy. Their long list of excuses has dwindled drastically. Lost in the mail? Just fax me a duplicate copy. Broken copy machine? Modem it to me. Or overnight it. Or call and record the relevant information on my voice mail.

If we don't want to apply ourselves from a pure motive of becoming better people, we should at least consider doing so for self-preservation.

Those who plan ahead and take action early can attest to the benefits of lower stress, more control over life, and the ability to confront their work with pleasure instead of with panic. You may never become one of those people who schedules all his or her doctor and dental checkups for the new year by January 1. But maybe you can get beyond thinking, *Another tooth gone. I may need to see a dentist one of these days.*

Finally, we must realize that every action we take (or don't take) affects our reputations in one way or the other. It takes a lifetime of conscientious acts to build a trustworthy reputation, but a single careless action can destroy one. So if you want to take advantage of this bit of wisdom, act now.

BLURRED VISION

Control your dislike of others. We often indulge in instinctively disliking certain people before we even know anything about them. Sometimes this spontaneous yet regrettable tendency includes prominent people. Even as admiration of great leaders reflects well on us, dislike of them degrades us.

When you see someone for the first time, what does it take to create an instant impression—either positive or negative? Consider some of these possibilities: body piercing, a foreign or Southern accent, a Metallica T-shirt, a Bible, black lipstick and fingernail polish, a tattoo, a wheelchair, body odor, a pro-choice button, a GOP campaign hat, etc.

Sometimes we only get this far and never get around to realizing there is a person beneath those clothes, smells, sounds, and physical features. We are so preconditioned to react to certain stereotypes that we never allow the person opportunity to prove us wrong. If we get past what we see, what we hear might put us off. If not, what we smell might.

This is not to suggest that you approach a large man in full gang regalia, running out of a liquor store with a pistol in one hand and wads of cash in the other, and offer him a hug. But neither should you allow this one instance to make you suspicious of everyone who is large, wears that particular color clothing, runs, owns a gun, or handles cash. If you do, it's only a matter of time until you are "tsk-tsking" anyone who wears brown shoes with a suit or parts his hair on the right instead of the left.

In addition, when we become so sensitive to the way other people look, we can seldom prevent becoming somewhat paranoid about ourselves. When we are hasty to judge someone based solely on appearance, we suspect others are doing the same thing to us. It quickly becomes a miserable way to live.

We must not allow insignificant things to cause temporary nearsightedness. If our vision is blurred, let it be on the externals, so we are better able to focus on the real person just beyond them. That person just might turn out to be a sight for sore eyes.

A ROLL OF THE DICE?

Know how to make good choices. The course of your life depends on this. You need both discrimination and judgment, for which pure intelligence is not sufficient. You need first to know how to choose—and then choose the best option. There are many who have strong minds, keen judgment, great learning, and still cannot make a decision. Being able to choose the best course is the greatest of gifts.

As soon as you walk into a restaurant, you start making decisions:

> Table or booth?
>
> Smoking or nonsmoking?
>
> Breakfast or lunch menu?
>
> What will you order?
>
> Soup or salad?
>
> What kind of dressing?
>
> Ya want fries with that?
>
> Will you be having dessert?

Some people agonize over choices even at this simple level. How many times have you been out to eat when someone at the table weighed every option, debated between the two or three top choices, sought advice from others, and still wasn't satisfied with his or her ultimate choice? Others become quite casual with their choices. They close their eyes and point to something on the menu. Toss a coin. Take the waitperson's first recommendation. Whatever.

It's true that the choice matters little in a restaurant—prices and allergies aside. But in other concerns, each of these decision-making styles can create problems. Suppose rather than deciding between beef or chicken, the person is deciding between a legal career or the ministry. The difficulty of such a choice might keep an insecure person debating, seeking advice, and weighing options until retirement. (Of course, insecure people may not belong in either a pastorate or legal practice.) On the other hand, who wants a lawyer or minister who got there as a result of a coin toss?

It's prudent to use deeper levels of wisdom when faced with tough decisions. Making the choice is the first challenge. But choosing well is just as important—if not more so. You can take this advice, or you can go on as casually as you have in the past. The choice is yours.

BRAIN POWER VS. WILLPOWER

You need to be both hard working and intelligent. Diligence promptly carries out what bright minds conceive. Fools move quickly because they don't perceive the obstacles and don't prepare. Yet the wise can fail by procrastination. Too much knowledge may make one overly cautious. Leave nothing until tomorrow. In other words, "Make haste carefully."

Have you ever heard of Mycroft Holmes? He was a minor character in the writings of Sir Arthur Conan Doyle. In fact, Mycroft was Sherlock Holmes's older (and smarter) brother. But since the cerebral Mycroft was all concentration and little application, the protagonist of Doyle's stories was always Sherlock. It was Sherlock who caught the bad guys, who recovered stolen valuables, and who foiled the evil Professor Moriarty. His IQ might not have been on par with Mycroft's, but Sherlock was the hero by demonstrating diligence and taking action.

Being intelligent comes naturally to some. Others must work hard to access information and comprehend difficult concepts. Yet it's not so much what goes into the mind but what comes out in practical applications that is important. And a big part of being practical is pacing one's time and effort.

Many of us approach every challenge of life at a sprint. We move from one short burst to the next, going all out each time, looking good, but getting more winded with each new ordeal. It doesn't matter how determined you are. It doesn't matter that you give it all you've got. It doesn't matter that you're wise and have good intentions. If you approach life at a sprint, you'll be like any runner trying to sprint through a marathon. You will run out of steam long before you're ready, resulting in failure and frustration.

In order to "make haste carefully," you need wisdom and stamina. Many past difficulties become "elementary" when you learn to combine Sherlock's diligence with the patience and pacing of a marathon runner. So get out there and get going. The game is afoot!

GOTTA HAVE IT . . . NOW!

Know how to wait. Never be in a hurry to let your passions control you. Master yourself before you manage others. You will travel through cycles of time before opportunity strikes. Fortune is the reward of the one who waits.

How many times have you let your passions maneuver you into an impulse purchase, only to discover a much better deal the following week? Suppose, for example, you are beginning to shop for a computer. You might find a model with exactly the features and memory you desire, yet you don't need the machine for several months. In the computer industry, a few months are a lifetime. Six months from now, much more advanced models will be available. Yet if the exact one you need has been available for a while, you should be able to get an excellent bargain.

The same is true of cars, athletic shoes, and many other high-ticket items that tend to change styles regularly. If we could only learn to control those pesky passions, we could get a lot more for our money.

And if we could control our passions in life, we could vastly improve our time investments and relationships.

Just as some people try to diminish anger by counting to ten whenever offended, the same technique works to diffuse potential harm that our passions might cause.

Live television programs frequently use a time delay of several seconds "just in case." If an exuberant celebrity lets an offensive word or phrase slip, the producer can act quickly and delete the offensive words. Thanks to the time delay, a passionate expression can be tempered for the good of all involved. Similarly, we can voluntarily develop a time delay between feeling a passionate urge and acting on it.

In life, we control "time delay."

ALL THE WAY

Make sure that your efforts succeed in the end. Some are more concerned about the stress of the moment than winning itself. Yet in the eyes of others, the discredit of failing at the last moment cancels recognition for the hard work previously completed. The victor does not need explanations.

Time ran out for someone in April 1995. A winning ticket in the Michigan lottery went unclaimed and the holder lost out on $2.4 million. It makes you wonder what happened. Was it lost? Or could it be that someone regularly shelled out money in hopes of hitting it big, only to neglect checking the winning numbers each time?

As we read such stories, questions arise about other potential losses—losses that perhaps are even more devastating. When you examine your life, can you identify any areas where you've invested much time and/or money yet aren't seeing the process through to a productive end? Consider some of the following possibilities:

Do you have an unpublished book or story that you're reluctant to show to anyone?

Can you play a musical piece that you might perform in public if you could just work out a particularly difficult passage?

Could you graduate or get another degree if you would just take another course or write your dissertation?

If you took on just a little more responsibility, could you get a raise and/or promotion at work?

Many people initially devote a lot of energy to projects such as these yet never receive the benefits that come at completion. Perhaps it bothers them more to let a 50-percent-off coupon to their favorite restaurant expire than to deny others their unique gifts or talents due to shyness, laziness, or fear.

We must move forward until we cross the finish line. The pace may not always be what we'd like it to be, but the journey will be much more worthwhile.

IN YOUR PRIME

Do not drain anything to the dregs. A wise man once stated that all virtue was found in the golden mean, or in avoiding extremes. Push anything to its far limits and it becomes distorted; press all the juice from an orange and it shrivels.

If you're ever out hiking in the country and come upon a pump with a little jar of water beside it, don't drink the water. Even if you were very thirsty, you would not be wise to drink from the jar. Instead, slowly pour the water into the pump as you pump the handle up and down. Soon you should have a rushing torrent of fresh, cold water—much superior to what was in the jar. Drink all you want and then fill up the jar for the next person.

You may be thinking, *It doesn't take a genius to know this.* Yet instead of a pump, what if the same principle is applied to your employees, your spouse, your family? Do you regularly prime the pump to keep them at their very best and freshest? Or are you pumping a dry well, so to speak?

You can look at people walking down the street and frequently tell which ones have been drained to the dregs. Many people struggle with their self-image. They have intense family problems. And when they get to work, perhaps they have an employer who feels it is his job to squeeze out every last drop of creativity, initiative, and devotion.

Each of us either adds to the problems of those with whom we come into contact, or we lighten their loads. Every interaction gently pushes the other person one way or the other.

When you start relating to those around you rather than being overly demanding, you'll discover it's something to get pumped up about.

A SKELETON-FREE CLOSET

Seek and maintain a good reputation. You pay a high price for a solid reputation, for it is linked with unusual abilities. These are as rare as mediocrity is common. When it is obtained through great applied talents or noble deeds, it is almost held in awe by others and carries a certain majesty. Only a solid reputation that is proven lasts indefinitely.

Daniel the prophet is usually remembered in association with his night in the lions' den. Yet God's protection of Daniel was no more or less spectacular than it was for numerous other people. The truly outstanding thing about Daniel is that he had 122 people watching his every move, determined to catch him doing something wrong. But they couldn't. The Bible says, "They could find no corruption in [Daniel], because he was trustworthy and neither corrupt nor negligent" (Daniel 6:4).

Daniel maintained a good reputation. When he was nominated for high office, no one could find any skeletons in his closet, no matter how hard they looked or how far back they went. How many politicians today can make the same claim?

A reputation cannot be quickly built or rebuilt. Someone who wants to improve his or her reputation must commit to a long and challenging effort to overcome previous shortcomings. You may never be required to demonstrate great applied talents or perform noble deeds, but you'll be expected to do the right thing over and over again if you want to solidify your reputation.

Of course, having a spotless reputation isn't always all it's cracked up to be. It didn't keep Daniel out of the lions' den. When Daniel's detractors couldn't find anything legitimate to pin on him, they set him up and let him take the fall in their scam. That's when God stepped in and took care of him.

Daniel did his part. God did His. Are you doing yours?

INNOCENT BY ASSOCIATION

Only associate with honorable people. You can both trust each other. Their honor is the best guarantee of pure intentions even in misunderstanding. You cannot deal with deceitful people, for a sense of honesty will not hold them hostage. There can be no true friendship or binding agreements with them because they have no sense of honor. Without honor, virtue is impossible.

An old song tells of a drunkard who is sleeping it off in a gutter when a pig comes by and decides to join him for a nap. A woman of high society passes and comments: "You can tell the one who boozes by the company he chooses." In response, the pig gets up and walks away.

Like it or not, we are judged by the company we keep. If we associate with honorable people, others will conclude that we, too, are honest and upright. If we hang out with thieves, the assumption will be made that we cannot be completely trusted. The assumptions may or may not be correct in either case, yet they will exist.

We can't always determine what other people think about us. We do, however, get to choose our own thoughts and opinions, so it's too bad when we choose to involve ourselves in close relationships where we cannot think the best about the other people. If you know that a friend gossips about all your other associates, can you believe that he or she doesn't do so about you as well? If your business partner boasts of sticking it to the IRS on his personal tax return, how do you feel when he then begins to file for your company? When someone promises to do something "on my honor," what can you do when you realize he or she is not an honorable person?

We cannot avoid coming into contact with certain people who take advantage or cause problems for us. Yet we can determine to what degree we get involved with them. If a fiancé proves untrustworthy, we need not feel compelled to go through with the marriage. If a prospective partner at work is involved in questionable accounting practices, his promotion can be postponed. Maintaining honor requires making hard decisions. Of course, as we spend more time with honorable people, those decisions become a bit easier each time.

AN AGE OF EASY CREDIT

Do not make a great deal about small things. Some talk big, take everything seriously, and turn ordinary things into disputes. Troublesome things should not be taken too seriously, if possible. The remedy may be worse than the disease. One of life's important lessons is to let things alone if you are able.

Modern society tends to rewrite time-tested proverbs and adages. It used to be that we were taught to "give credit where credit is due." These days, however, it seems as if people live by the creed, "Take credit whenever you can."

A reporter gets an anonymous call exposing a political scandal but takes all the credit for breaking the story. A celebrity hires a writer to put together an autobiography that makes the best-seller list but takes full credit for writing it on all the talk shows and at book signings. A job applicant talks of running the previous company, inflating every minor accomplishment.

Other people regularly inflate small things like their aches and pains. When you see them coming, you quickly head the opposite direction so you won't have to spend a half-hour or more hearing about migraines, muscle pulls, and other ailments that would put a pro-football player out of commission.

How refreshing it is to be around people who downplay the significance of their accomplishments, their problems, and their opinions. Indeed, if we ever find such people, we seek out their thoughts. Whatever it is that allows them to operate without calling attention to themselves is appealing, whether it's humility, timidity, or something else. It is perceived as wisdom, and it works in their favor.

It is frequently noted that the squeaky wheel gets the grease. True. But after a few costly trips to the garage to be treated with the grease gun, if the wheel continues to squeak, it is likely to be replaced. As another time-tested proverb says, "A word to the wise is sufficient."

WHEN IT DOESN'T PAY TO BE FRANK

Make yourself indispensable. There are ways to be rewarded by favor from others. The best way is to excel in your occupation and talents and add a pleasant disposition. You will become essential to your position, rather than your position defining you. Some do honor their calling, but with others, less successful, the opposite is true.

*M*A*S*H* remains one of the most popular programs in television history. One of its strongest points was its cast of characters. Benjamin Franklin (Hawkeye) Pierce was a central figure. He was the 4077's indispensable surgeon. In stark contrast to Hawkeye was Frank Burns, a higher ranking officer, yet far less qualified as a doctor.

Because of his expertise in the OR, Hawkeye regularly earned the respect of his fellow soldiers. He could get by with more than his share of mischief in other areas, because whenever he got into trouble, people were eager to assist him. Frank, on the other hand, was barely tolerated, and his problems meant little to others.

Hawkeye Pierce was not always a model of pleasant disposition, yet he proves that anyone who excels in life will be noticed. And if that person is also pleasant and caring, he or she will have friends in abundance.

Do you honor your calling? Has your vocation become a daily grind, or do you regularly set higher goals and create new challenges to remain enthused? Does your position define and limit who you are, or do you continually expand the parameters and become an essential employee?

Any Frank-Burns-type can pull rank. Yet it is far better to prove your point with extraordinary skill and dedication. You may be outranked. You may be outnumbered. But if you know you're right, don't give up. Some days your extra effort won't seem worthwhile. But over a lifetime, you'll be amazed at the difference.

WOULD YOU LIKE TO SEE A WHINE LIST?

Never complain. It will always bring you disfavor. It is better to be a model of self-reliance than an object of someone else's pity. By complaining of past offenses, we open the door to new ones. If we are shrewd, we will never tell the world of our failures or defeats without showing how we overcame them.

One two-letter word holds volumes of meaning:

> *If* I had his money, I could do big things.

> *If* I hadn't gotten sick, I would have won the sales contest.

> *If* my parents had loved me more, I wouldn't be so messed up.

> *If* my children loved me more, I wouldn't be such a nervous wreck.

Yeah. And if you had a nickel for every time someone used an *if* clause to complain about his or her life, you could retire wealthy right now.

Complaints and excuses fill the lives of some people. Nothing is ever good enough. No one is ever loving enough. No meal is tasty enough. No report is clear enough. No benefit is adequate enough. No book or movie is entertaining enough. And rather than endure the least little disappointment, it seems to be the person's choice of therapy to whine loud and long.

The problem with complaining is that it does no good. Certainly a person has every right to go "on record" by disagreeing with personal opinions, policies, and such. But when overruled or outvoted, then the person needs to be a bit more gracious and less vocal.

Note the subtle effects of complaining: Friendships dissolve. People actually pity us. And once the cycle of complaining begins, life only gets worse and worse. Think about it. To what lengths will you go to avoid spending time or working with someone who is a chronic complainer?

By all means, change the things you can to make your surroundings a better place. But when you can't do anything, keep your complaints to yourself. Whining is worthless. Silence, on the other hand, can be golden.

HERRING AIDS

Look into the heart of things. Matters are generally different than they first appear. Lies come first and truth lags behind at the end, limping on the arm of time. Those who are ignorant are often disillusioned when the kernel of things is exposed. Yet the wise, when listening to others, always hold back one ear which they reserve for truth.

People who read mysteries know to watch out for "red herrings"—false leads, miscues, or anything that draws attention from the real issue. The reference is derived from a hunting term. If hounds are pursuing a fox, someone might drag a red herring across the trail. The fish scent does wonders to confuse the poor hounds and buys the fox some time.

What fun would a mystery be if the killer confessed in the first chapter? Indeed, the more cunning the criminal, the more wily the investigator must be. We admire the detecting skills of our fictional heroes: the Hardy Boys, Nancy Drew, Miss Marple, Hercule Poirot, Mike Hammer, Charlie Chan, Nero Wolfe, and Sam Spade. The list goes on. The differences in the personalities, jobs, and physical appearances of these detectives are vast, yet the common bond they share is their ability to get past the red herrings and to the truth.

Truth is frequently elusive. We must follow its trail like hounds after a fox. There are plenty of people up ahead of us, fish in hand, trying to cover their tracks and keep the truth hidden. If we don't want to remain confused and deceived, we must rigorously pursue truth.

Life is filled with mysteries. The next time something smells fishy to you, you're probably getting close to a cover-up. Keep searching for the truth until you're back on the right trail. And happy hunting.

YESTERDAY-MORNING QUARTERBACKING

Think beforehand. Begin today to think about tomorrow. The best foresight consists of sensing coming trouble. Many act first and think later. They don't pay attention to possible consequences but only make excuses. Some don't even give serious thought before or after a mistake. All of your life should be focused on remaining on the right path.

Many of us who enjoy professional football may never consider the preparation and work that go into the sport. Physical strength and stamina are certainly a concern, yet most coaches will tell you that the biggest challenge is keeping the players' heads in the game.

To a novice, it may seem that a team's offense is a matter of run, run, pass, punt—over and over again. Yet the play calls are far from random. Coaches and players study game films (their own and those of other teams). They want to analyze themselves to detect mistakes that can be avoided in the future and to prepare for every contingency. They pore over other teams' films in search of weaknesses, predictable calls, and anything that might give them an edge. When game day comes, it may not be the stronger team that wins but the one who is more prepared.

It may feel as if your first step out of bed in the morning is a step onto a field where everyone is out to get you. This can be true whether you're a corporate CEO, a private in military service, a mother of a jelly-faced toddler, or any number of roles. Perhaps you have committed to give it all you've got each and every day. If so, it's a noble sentiment, yet you could take a lesson from your favorite football team. The game doesn't begin when you step onto the field but the night, the week, and the months beforehand. Very likely, the amount of forethought and preparation you devote to any effort will be the factor that determines its success or failure.

There was a reason your teachers used to tell you not to cram for tests just before taking them. The preferred method of study is regular involvement with the material and a more intensive review the night before the exam. After you sleep on it, you're ready to go the next morning.

You can expect a number of tests tomorrow. What are you doing today to prepare for them?

NO LAUGHING MATTER

Do not make mistakes about the character of others. This can be a fatal error. In dealing with people, rather than things, we must look at the heart. It takes a strong philosophical sense to prove depths of interactions and perceive traits of character. People should be studied as deeply as books.

We all know that character assassination is bad, but is it really a "fatal error"?

A high-school referee officiated at a state playoff game between two small schools—both undefeated. The game went into overtime before one team finally won. Naturally, the losing team questioned some of the referee's calls along the way, but from there the situation got out of control. The referee lived sixty-five miles away, but a carload of fans followed him home from the game and staked out his house. The media played back every questionable play from the game in slow motion. Calls and letters began to come in, even from parents and teachers, that questioned his integrity and concern for young people. A state association relieved his crew from future games at which they had been scheduled to officiate.

As a result of all these things, the thirty-six-year-old referee tried to kill himself. The attempt was not successful and he is all right today, yet he might tell you that what occurred was a serious misevaluation of his character.

We have learned to define certain people according to their jobs: referees, teachers, bosses, politicians, TV evangelists, etc. Worse yet, perhaps we pay too much attention to TV comedians and define these people according to their faults and foibles. We may not like these targets of criticism or what they are doing, yet we dare not forget that first and foremost they are *people*.

People should be studied as books. Yet when we consider what kinds of titles make the best-seller lists these days, we need to give people much greater consideration than flash-in-the-pan books. And we need to remember not to judge them by their covers.

IN DEED I DO

Be able to tell the difference between people of mere words and those with deeds. Bad words even without bad deeds are poor enough, but good words combined with bad deeds are worse. One cannot profit from words which are mere wind. Politeness is often polite deceit. Words should be the pledges of deeds. Fig trees that bear leaves but no fruit have little value.

"I'll get back to you after lunch."

"You can count on me."

"Hey, I owe you one!"

We all hear these promises from numerous people, but how can we tell which ones really mean what they promise? Time always tells. Those who actually do what they say earn points toward the next promise they make or the next favor they request. People who make empty promises to earn favor or stall for time, and who never get around to following through, only hurt themselves.

This is an area where it's easy to see the short-comings of other people while overlooking one's own.

For example, consider the following statements you may have made lately:

> "Thanks for all your help. I appreciate your support."

> "I'm proud to be your mother (or father)."

> "I love you."

> "Let's have dinner soon."

> "We'll spend time together when I get home. I promise."

This list could go on, but you get the idea. You've put the words out there in the wind, but are they really pledges of your deeds? They won't be until you actually do something about them. Even the best intentions won't get the job done.

People die every day, leaving behind good intentions and broken promises. But it's the people who do what they say and demonstrate their words with actions who have truly learned to live.

A SIMPLER TIME?

Do not live in a hurry. Many spend their fortunes before ending their lives. They fly through pleasures without really enjoying them. There should be moderation even in the search for knowledge—some things are better left alone. Be slow in enjoying life but swift at work. The end of work is pleasure, but pleasure is often completed with regret.

Perhaps you know people with immaculate homes filled with priceless works of art who never seem content. Maybe you know people who travel frequently, for work and/or pleasure, yet never seem to appreciate the places they've been or the sights they have seen. Such people seem to be eager to get somewhere but are never quite sure where they are going. Consequently, they will never know if they get there and will continue to search for some elusive, satisfying conclusion to all their efforts.

We need not possess the *Mona Lisa* to appreciate fine art. Most of us are in easy driving distance of an art museum with free (or at least reasonable) admission. You may feel frustrated if you do not live beside the ocean, in the shadow of the Rocky Mountains, or beneath the aurora borealis. But do you take advantage of the natural beauty that *does* surround you: sunrises, sunsets, snowfalls, the myriad of colors provided by the flowers on your block, the shade beneath that secluded grove of trees that only you know about?

The trouble is, we don't often slow down to see all that surrounds us. Therefore, we're rarely happy. In our desire to be somewhere else or acquire something new, we miss out on so much we could appreciate. Live in the present, and your life will prove to be more pleasurable to you.

BETTER DISCRETION THAN DISGRACE

Avoid being on a too-familiar basis with others. And don't let others become too familiar with you. The one who indulges in familiarity may lose superiority and thus lose respect. In total communication, you relay the failings that reserved behavior would have kept hidden. We must use street-smart wisdom and really know and trust others before we take that risk. Avoid it with superiors because it is dangerous and with inferiors because it is unbecoming.

One of the memorable events of Jimmy Carter's presidency was the flak he received after honestly admitting to a member of the press that, on occasion, he was not completely free of impure thoughts. His confession to having "lust in my heart" was the topic of discussion for weeks to follow.

Essentially, all President Carter was saying was that he was not above having the same temptations and potential weaknesses of any other man. It's just that most people didn't want to know that much about him. We tend to put our leaders on pedestals—at least we used to. Consequently, we hold them to a higher level of expectation than we set for ourselves.

Most experienced business leaders or pastors now regret that they shared too much personal information earlier in their careers. For example, a minister might make it known that he was something of a wild teenager before becoming a Christian. The image of this "man of God" involved in an era of free love, pot smoking, and Jimi Hendrix music may be too much for some people to handle. As far as the pastor is concerned, his past is a matter of confessed and forgiven sin, but he has had years to mature. In the hands of immature or disillusioned churchgoers, the secret past of the pastor is likely to resurface in various forms of disdain and innuendo.

Wise leaders learn appropriate levels of openness and vulnerability to use around people at various stages of maturity. Certainly, we shouldn't lie to people or plan a lifelong covert operation to hide every mistake or unpopular opinion. It's simply wise not to become too familiar. One or two seemingly insignificant revelations is all it takes to undo a lot of hard work and accumulated respect. So the next time you have lust in your heart, you may want to keep it to yourself.

WIELDING POWER VS. YIELDING POWER

Do not hold on to your opinions too firmly. Every foolish person is firmly convinced. Even in some cases of obvious certainty in your opinion, it is all right to yield. Our reason for holding a particular view may be recognized but so will our courtesy in yielding to others. Steadfast qualities should relate more to the will than the mind, although it is important to be correct in judgment and practice.

The story is told of a naval ship forced to sail through an unexpected and violent storm. In the midst of the fray, radar picked up a large object nearby, and visual checks, though hazy, confirmed a light dead ahead. The captain sent an immediate message: "Change your course to avoid impact." The reply came back: "Cannot comply. Advise you change course instead."

An admiral who happened to be on the ship took over, sending the message: "This is Admiral Jones on a United States warship. Advise you change your position immediately." The reply was convincing: "Sir, just this once, we suggest you yield. We are a lighthouse."

Sometimes our place in the company pyramid just doesn't matter. Our strongest opinions and assumptions might be wrong. As accustomed as we might be to getting our way, we should learn when to yield to others' opinions—sometimes out of expediency and sometimes when the outcome isn't important. Otherwise we develop the mentality of an Internet chat room where people are hotly debating the leadership skills of *Star Trek's* Captain Kirk opposed to Captain Picard or the sex appeal of *Gilligan's Island* characters Ginger versus Mary Ann. So what if you have a strong opinion? It simply doesn't matter whether or not others come around to your way of thinking.

Always know what is right and hold to your beliefs. But in cases where truth isn't an issue and all that exists are opinions, four words can save hours of valuable time and a lot of grief: "You may be right."

SEE THROUGH LEADERS

Be able to recognize faults, even in prominent people. Your integrity can uncover vices, even among the wealthy, intelligent, and famous. As an analogy, slavery does not lose its vile qualities because it is disguised by the nobility of the master. If a great man has great faults, he is not great because of them. Those who flatter the great often gloss over faults they abhor in those of lesser stature.

Hans Christian Andersen's *The Emperor's New Clothes* is a perfect illustration of this principle. If we ignore the blatant faults of those we supposedly respect, they look foolish and so do we. It took the refreshing honesty of a young child to point out that the emperor was strolling down the street stark naked. The mature and informed adults weren't willing to acknowledge the obvious.

We need more of that blunt honesty today. We seem to be hard-pressed for heroes, so we make do with what we have. We turn to sports figures and are crushed when they are exposed in scandals involving drugs or gambling. We turn to entertainers, only to see too many destroyed too soon from lifestyles of excess or by their own hand. We turn to politicians and are dismayed to discover how many are not the virtuous people they present themselves to be. We may finally turn to the church, only to find that even many of those leaders aren't as upstanding as we'd imagined them to be.

It's not that we should stop seeking out genuine heroes. The point is, in our admiration of others, we dare not ignore their foibles or all-out character flaws. If your best friend had the same personality, he or she wouldn't be your friend for long. So why overlook the faults of someone who is prominent, powerful, and influential? If you do, you're going to be embarrassed the next time your "emperor" gets caught with his pants down.

LOOK BOTH WAYS

Have an objective view of yourself and your life. In the beginning, everyone has high hopes and dreams. Yet experience may not fulfill idle imaginations. The wise man anticipates the best but expects the worst. It is wise to aim high to hit your target but not so high that you miss your mission at the outset. If you understand your true calling, you'll reconcile ideals with reality.

Charles Dickens began his *A Tale of Two Cities* with a classic opening: "It was the best of times, it was the worst of times." He seemed to understand the truth in acknowledging the extremes of life.

Some motivational speakers would have us limit our perceptions. If we "expect the worst," they say, we'll get it. The inference is that if we keep stars in our eyes and think only happy thoughts, we can avoid anything truly unpleasant. This assumption is naive at best, dangerous at worst.

Establish high hopes and dreams. Anticipate the best. When you're making plans, aim high. Optimism is a valuable mind-set as long as you don't let reality get away from you. If you're fifty-seven and still get queasy at the sight of blood, you may want to give up that dream to become a brain surgeon. If your budget begins to restrict your goal to visit every country in the world, you need not give up your love for travel. Instead of glumly mourning what you can't do, get out and do what you can.

Hopes and dreams may suffer when confronted with the realities of life, yet they may not need to die altogether. When we're small children, we are taught to look both ways before crossing a street. Our wise teachers and parents realize that things may appear sunny and safe in one direction, even while a crazed madman (or teenager with a learner's permit) approaches from the other. The street-smart kid will check all directions for danger signs. Yet with a small bit of patience and proper timing, he can safely get where he wants to go. And with similar determination and practice, so can you.

LIVING IN 3-D

Reality and appearances differ dramatically. Things are taken for granted for what they seem to be, not for what they are in reality. If your actions are correct but they appear otherwise, remember that few people can see your motives and intentions.

If you've ever worn those funny glasses to watch a 3-D movie, you know in your mind that the screen is only two-dimensional, yet it seems that objects are flying out toward you. You spend two hours dodging bullets and other projectiles. You duck when a punch is thrown in your direction. You scream when it seems certain you'll be struck by some of the cinematic debris. Though you know better, it's almost impossible to keep from reacting to the illusion of danger.

Appearances may be quite different from reality. This is especially true when people and personalities get involved. The person who smiles and shakes your hand might be a con man willing to take your last cent, while your scowling neighbor might turn out to be a valuable friend if you are willing to break the ice and reach out to her.

How about you? You can't do much to prevent someone else from sending out confusing signals, but you can work on your own methods of communication. Do you ever say yes when you really mean no—and then resent the other person for asking? Do you "keep up a brave face" when in front of people but go home and cry? Do you take whatever the boss dishes out to you and then take it out on the next person you see? If so, don't be surprised if other people take for granted what things seem to be.

When we attempt to live in three dimensions, yet reveal only two to others, we distort their vision. If we want their perception to be closer to reality, we have only one option. Since no one has yet invented glasses that help others see the depth of personality, it is up to us to let others witness more authenticity in our lives. The effect might be a bit scary at first, but they'll soon learn to enjoy the thrill.

REAL SMART BUT NOT SO BRIGHT

Intelligence can only bring us halfway to success. It is only one of the two sides of our ability. Strong character needs to be combined with it. The person without good character will fail in achieving stature in his career, community, and friendships.

In the spring of 1995, scandals were rocking the Ivy League. A Yale student, a month away from getting his diploma, was discovered to have forged his admittance transcripts. The college planned to not only expel him but also to press larceny charges. Meanwhile at Harvard, the administration was rescinding an offer of admittance to a young woman who was discovered to have bludgeoned her mother to death with a candlestick five years previously. She had lied about this incident during her interview.

There is no doubt that both of these students were brilliant. The girl had an IQ of 150. The guy had been a mediocre student at his community college yet maintained a B average at Yale. Neither problem was a question of intelligence but of character.

Similar character issues haunt the reputations of some of the most brilliant people who ever lived.

Character-related matters come to light about public figures on a regular basis—sex scandals, suicide, greed, and the like.

We cannot allow ourselves to be deceived in a similar manner. You can have the IQ of a genius. You can be a straight-A student and a high achiever at work. But that's just half the challenge. If you don't also strive to be a person with an impeccable reputation and a reputable character, then you're just plain wasting your superior intelligence.

CONVERSATION STARTLERS

Develop relationships with those who can teach you about life. Turn conversations with friends into instructive lessons. Though you are applauded for your own wisdom, you gain even more from what you hear from others. You can even learn from the students who surround the wisest of men.

Over thousands of hedges in thousands of yards between thousands of neighbors, the same conversation is taking place: "Some weather we're having, huh?" A slight variation takes place during thousands of coffee breaks: "How about those Bulls?" And even among those to whom we are closest, conversation frequently resorts to: "So how was your day today, dear?"

Neighbors, coworkers, and loved ones have much more to offer us than we take advantage of. If we could get past the weather, perhaps we would discover the fascinating lives and talents our neighbors have to share with us. If sports were not such a hot topic, we might find that coworkers are good for more than getting the latest project completed. And as well as spouses think they know each other, on any given day they can surprise each other with startling stories and encouragement.

Everyone is an expert at something. People tend to immerse themselves in hobbies and skills and may seem modest about sharing them with others. Yet if someone is willing to gently prod them about their interests, a wealth of information is available.

A lot of fuss is being made about the information pipeline available on computer screens. But we don't even take advantage of the potential information with which we come into contact every day. Every handshake or nod of greeting is a new opportunity to discover something interesting and life changing. Unless, of course, you feel a pressing need to discuss the weather.

IRON CAN'T SHARPEN PUTTY

Surround yourself with people who have great knowledge in order to protect yourself from your own ignorance and help you get out of the difficulties that stem from it. We have little time to live but much to learn. If wise people can't work for you, at least have them as friends.

On a scale of one (least) to ten (most), how much would you say you are committed to continued learning? Now that school, homework, and report cards are behind you, have you stopped learning as well?

It's natural to have a "no more teachers, no more books" attitude for a few days after hanging a diploma on your wall. But this mentality is dangerous if it continues. We need an eagerness to learn—not just formal book learning but from those around us.

However, you probably know certain people who surround themselves with inferiors who are easily intimidated. Such people won't hire someone who appears too promising. They won't play golf with people better than themselves. They choose non-threatening friends whom they can regale with witty stories.

Meanwhile, they are never sufficiently challenged by anyone around them.

The Bible summarizes this matter succinctly: "As iron sharpens iron, so one man sharpens another" (Proverbs 27:17). It is the friction of thought, opinion, and passion between people that creates sparks of inspiration and wisdom. A person's IQ or job title matters little if he or she refuses to admit there is still considerable room for growth.

Our challenge is to be as sharp as we can be as individuals. Then we must interact with other equally sharp (or even sharper) people to continue to keep an edge. If we let our minds go to putty, no amount of sharpening is going to help.

IMAGINE THAT!

Keep your imagination under control. Sometimes you need to restrain it and sometimes enhance it. It should always be in harmony with your reasoning abilities. To some it promises happiness, to others, only grief. Control it so it will not delude you.

One of the more memorable television shows of the 1970s was *Fantasy Island*. Each week a plane full of guests would fly to the island where their host, Mr. Roarke, went to great lengths to ensure their every fantasy was fulfilled. Ironically, many of the episodes showed that people who lived out their fantasies were not nearly as satisfied as they had hoped to be. They discovered it was the spontaneity of life that brought happiness, not the luxury of guaranteeing all their dreams came true.

Imagination can be a wonderful gift. Of course, like any other gift it can either be used incorrectly or handled with care. Some people promote the use of imagination as a panacea of wisdom. Just visualize yourself a success, and you'll be a success. You are what you think you are. Use the power of your mind to recall past lives, walk on coals, bring about health and healing, etc.

Imagination should always be in harmony with your reasoning abilities. It should complement reason, not replace it altogether. You can imagine yourself to be Queen of England all you want, but it's just not going to happen (with one exception).

Happiness is not to be found on Fantasy Island. It is far better to keep your feet firmly planted on Reality Realty. Set up camp and get comfortable. Then let your imagination work for you. Know when to use it and when to lose it.

You don't have to imagine this will work—try it and find out for yourself.

CAN'T YOU TAKE A HINT?

Know how to take a hint. It is not enough to simply be able to use your reason. You need intuition, especially where you are most easily deceived. The things that matter most are only partially spoken; you need your complete effort to grasp the full meaning.

Something happens to most people between childhood and adulthood that diminishes their love for games. Most kids like puzzle games that challenge their minds. They can spend hours struggling with word searches, riddles, scrambled words, and other mind benders. And if they get stuck, they don't want the answer. They prefer a clue that will get them unstuck and on the way to solving the mystery themselves. "C'mon, Daddy, give me a hint!"

Adults, on the other hand, seem to lose this drive to solve problems. We prefer easy answers. Even worse, we stop recognizing hints when we get them. But sometimes it's embarrassing or uncomfortable for other people to spell out the entire truth for us, and we need to pick up on their clues.

For example, if your company is downsizing and your boss (who lives next door) doesn't include you when planning next year's carpool schedule, that might be a hint. If your work keeps you from seeing your daughter over extended periods of time during which she writes a report on why Little Orphan Annie is her favorite character, that might be a hint. If your spouse leaves travel brochures lying around a month before your anniversary, that might be a hint.

If you're ever puzzled because people are acting mysteriously, perhaps it is more your problem than theirs. Start looking for clues. If you use your head *and* your intuition, you're likely to find an abundance of them.

FOLLOWER CONFIDENCE

Those who have inborn leadership skills don't rely on mere cleverness but on the natural ability to govern. Others submit to this power without knowing why. These leaders are both lions and kings, inspiring the hearts and minds of those they lead.

Imagine a major battle is to be fought tomorrow. The leader of your forces is not confident in his abilities and is attempting to solicit support among the troops. Some he bribes with cash—half now and the rest after the victory. Others he attempts to coerce through guilt (You owe me one!), shame (What are you, chicken?), creating a sense of competition (You don't want the other units to have a better record, do you?), begging, convincing them what a nice guy he is, appealing to their patriotism, and so forth.

Under all the pressures of battle the next day, as the blood and bullets start to appear, how many followers do you think will remain loyal to the leader if they get an opportunity to escape unnoticed? Unless they are confident in the abilities of their leader, most are likely to go AWOL.

Followers need to trust their leaders. Good leaders know this and do all in their power to be trustworthy. However, mediocre leaders realize this as well. In the absence of experience and developed skills, they may attempt to substitute other extrinsic benefits. And indeed, raises and promotions may keep some a bit longer if the battle conditions of work aren't too terrible. But only genuine leaders will continue to motivate their followers and elicit their best work when the pressure is on.

It's hard to define exactly what combination of qualities comprises a good leader. Such gifted leaders usually seem to have the followers' best interests at heart. They both recognize and reward good work. They don't demand more of others than they do of themselves.

Think of some of the best leaders you know. Ask yourself: "What qualities does this person have that work so well for him or her? Why?" Even more importantly, try to figure out what you can do to improve your own abilities as a leader. Then, lead on.

PAYLOADS AND PAYOFFS

Don't take on the obligations of others. This is critical to being prudent in your affairs. It is easier to avoid committing yourself to something than it is to doing that same thing with excellence. One obligation may imply another and eventually lead to dishonor.

In the early days of NASA, people went out of their way to witness a missile launch. It was "high" drama. The stage was often set in the darkness of predawn. All was quiet for the spectators, though behind the scenes thousands of last-minute details were being verified. Then, finally, came the last seconds of the countdown . . . the fiery ignition . . . the gradual liftoff from the launch pad . . . the glorious ascension into the heavens.

One of the primary concerns during a launch, and a word that became more prevalent in our vocabularies, was payload—the combined weight of the passengers, instruments, and other things that weren't necessarily vital to making the rocket fly (such as fuel).

This concept of regulating payload is something we can apply to our lives as well. We all have a necessary amount of obligations to ourselves and to society, so we need to be careful how many additional obligations we take on. We certainly need to devote some of our excess time and energy to God, family, friends, and other essential relationships. Yet if we don't monitor the weight that such commitments place on us, we may find ourselves overburdened.

It is not coincidence that another word came into use during the space era: burnout. The NASA definition referred to the point at which the rockets cease to function. The heavier the payload, the quicker the burnout. But the nontechnical element of society quickly found a wider use of the word.

If you don't allow your payload to become excessive, you can fly high and experience the payoff for all your troubles. But try to carry too much, and you may not even get off the ground.

THE LAW IN THESE PARTS

Never lose your self-respect. Let your integrity be the true standard of all your actions. Your self-assessment should be stricter than the laws that govern human behavior. You should avoid evil because of your own strict standards over and above mere laws.

"In these parts, I'm the law."

It's a classic western line. One man stands between a cowering town and a gang of hostile outlaws. And while the town has certain rules on the books, the sheriff makes it clear in no uncertain terms that he has the authority to do whatever is necessary—law or no law—to protect those entrusted to his care.

Each of us has an obligation to protect the parts that have been assigned to us—hands that are tempted to steal when no one is looking, feet that threaten to take us places we ought not go, ears eager for malicious gossip, eyes that gaze on things that are better left unseen. There are laws that draw lines between what is permitted and what is punishable, yet those laws don't always slice cleanly between what is right and what is wrong. Regardless of what laws are on the books, you are the law in your parts. You have the final say in what is and isn't allowed.

We can spend our lives searching for loopholes to allow us to cross certain moral lines while remaining within the law. But is that really how we want to determine our actions? If so, life becomes more a matter of "getting away with stuff" rather than living according to the principles we believe in our hearts to be good and right and true.

We would do well to forget the code of the rest. What matters more is the internal code of conscience that keeps us focused on integrity. So when your temptations assemble and threaten to do damage to your reputation, stand firm. They'll be out of town by sundown.

ONE STRIKE AND YOU'RE OUT

Do not allow yourself to become upset. Losing control, or lack of prudence, will cause embarrassment. If you allow your passion to overflow into words, your reputation could be in danger. Let nothing disturb your composure, but enhance it by showing restraint.

Woody Hayes. Mention the name and some people immediately praise the Ohio State coach, one of the most notable leaders in the history of college football. But when the name is mentioned, other people say, "Isn't he the guy who hit the kid?"

In the intensity of an important game, a player from the other team was streaking down the sideline for a long and certain touchdown. Woody Hayes, unable to control himself, stepped from the sidelines onto the field and struck the player himself. It was an unthinkable act that occurred toward the end of a long and distinguished career, yet that one action became his legacy.

We can't be too tough on Coach Hayes. We've all been in a position of loss and frustration, desperate to persevere and rise to victory but helpless to do so. Maybe we've even taken desperate measures to remedy the situation, though our own drastic actions probably weren't captured on national television.

Learning to control our passions is more important than learning how not to get caught. Some states have passed laws guaranteed to imprison third-time convicted offenders. These "third strike" laws are frequently debated. Yet when it's your reputation on the line, you won't even get to the third strike. One mistake and your good reputation crumbles. Two, and it shatters.

Sometimes the other team is going to win, despite our best efforts. Sometimes we cannot determine the actions of those around us. Yet losing control only makes things worse. Wise people restrain themselves early. People who never learn this may eventually need other forms of restraint—like handcuffs. Self-restraint is difficult when you lose a game, promotion, or reward. But if you wait until others have to do the restraining, you stand to lose your good reputation as well.

TO DREAM THE POSSIBLE DREAM

Cultivate sound judgment. Appreciate the things of greatest importance. It is great fortune to associate with those of the highest taste. But do not be dissatisfied with everything else, for it is foolish to seek unreachable ideals.

Your preference of fine art might be the primitive style of Grandma Moses. It might be the impressionistic style of Monet. It might be the rearrangement of three-dimensional space used by Picasso or Dali. Then again, you might prefer dogs playing poker or Elvis on black velvet.

Each of these styles has merit of its own. We ought not limit our interests and relationships to only what involves the highest taste: Renaissance art, gourmet food, classical music, and such. Indeed, many people who prefer the classics become snobs toward those of "lesser" taste. And it's not uncommon to find common people who are reverse snobs toward those who don't appreciate bluegrass music or belt-buckle collections. If we open our minds to other kinds of cultural expression, it's hard to keep them closed toward other kinds of people.

The very reason we have so many kinds of art and music is because there are so many kinds of people. We aren't supposed to be alike. If you are ever fortunate enough to receive an invitation to the White House, you should feel honored and appreciate the experience. But don't feel slighted because you can't spend every night in the Lincoln bedroom.

Man of La Mancha, the musical based on *Don Quixote,* is the source of the ambitious song, "To Dream the Impossible Dream." We certainly need to have high goals and lofty dreams. Yet in the meantime, we need to be more content with what we do have—whether we live in the White House, Graceland, or a third-world country. We must remind ourselves to make the most of our waking hours and relationships. It would be a shame to dream them all away.

BE YOUR OWN MIKE

Choose a heroic ideal. There are many examples of greatness, living texts of honor. Don't just follow them; rather, let them spur you on to greater deeds. Nothing stirs up ambition as much as the trumpet call of someone else's fame. This should create a generous rather than an envious spirit.

Why do so many people admire Michael Jordan? Most of his fans will never come close to knowing the sensation of sailing though the air over a couple of defenders and effortlessly slamming the ball through the hoop. Yet Michael is a hero for people of all ages. One of the companies he sponsors even used the slogan, "I want to be like Mike," for product promotion.

As kids, we want to be like our heroes. We desire to pick up a basketball and become Michael, pick up a guitar and become Eric Clapton, or pick up a pen and become John Grisham. When we get old enough for reality to set in, we settle for being like our heroes. Yet we need to be careful what it is about our heroes that we admire.

It isn't productive to envy another person's talent. We can certainly admire it and be inspired by it, yet we shouldn't feel frustrated if we can't do everything the other person does. What we should do is let that person help motivate us to do better at whatever it is we can do. In order to "be like Mike," you may need to excel with a spatula rather than a basketball. You may need ballet shoes rather than Air Jordans. Your press might be at the laundry rather than on the court. But you can be sure that whatever you do, if you don't feel thrilled and fulfilled by doing it, you aren't being like Mike.

Heroes are not so often created by what they do as much as how they do it. Few skills come naturally. What we should admire are the ingredients of their success: commitment, practice, dedication, perseverance, and recovery from failure. These are helpful in spurring ourselves on to greater deeds. And if we stick with it, other people may consider some of those deeds downright heroic.

SUPPORTING ROLES

Be all things to all people. Learn the art of gaining everyone's support. Go with the moods of others, adapting to their changes without their notice. This is especially important if you are dependent upon them.

Doctors are specialists, but they can't perform surgery alone. They would have a much harder time performing any procedure without their nurses. All the doctor needs to do is name an instrument and the nurse instantly places it in his or her hand. Many times the nurse has it ready before the doctor even asks for it. The more that doctors and nurses depend upon each other and work well together, the better it is for the patient.

Now contrast this positive example of interdependency with that of a shifty politician running for office. He, too, is dependent upon others—in this case, to get elected. He becomes all things to all people. He craves everyone's support. The trouble is, he is likely to promise things he can't deliver or compromise his personal standards.

There's an art to gaining the support of others, but there's a discipline in being there for them as well. The more people who support us, the more time will be required in returning favors. Yet this is an important part of life. The added challenge is coming through for them even when we feel they don't deserve it. Back in the ER, the doctors sometimes get panicky and begin barking orders to the nurses. A good nurse will respond to the command, not the tone. When a heart has stopped and the person is turning blue is not the time to stop everything and declare, "I don't appreciate your attitude, Doctor."

Similarly, we need to be there for people even when they aren't as appreciative as they should be. Pain, fear, and other powerful emotions can cause nice people to act not so nicely. We need to see them through the emergency first. We can address our concerns about their attitudes later.

When you see someone in need, lend a hand. Later, when you find yourself in need, you may be surprised at how many hands are there to support you.

JOLLY GOOD

A cheerful disposition kept in balance is a positive, not a negative. Join in the fun, but preserve your dignity. Humor can get you out of tight spots. Take criticism in jest, even if others may mean it seriously.

Most married couples can attest to the value of a good laugh. Many can relate stories of arguments that quickly escalated into major fights, complete with name-calling, accusations, and worse. Then, unexpectedly, one person said or did something that made the other laugh. The slightest giggle at just the right time has incredible power to obliterate conflict. A knockdown, drag-out fight can immediately become an on-the-floor, laugh-filled reconciliation.

Most people prefer laughing to fighting. So why is it that so many of our relationships are marked by yelling instead of smiling, scowls instead of howls, and grimaces instead of guffaws? If the other person is reluctant to use humor and lighten up, the initiative is up to us.

If you believe that a cheerful disposition is impossible in your home or business, then that's exactly the place it is needed most. That's where humor will stand out.

Everyone smiles at Disneyland, so cheerfulness is taken for granted. Perhaps you have the opportunity to become an ambassador of humor in a grim and laughless place.

Yet humor must be paired with dignity. Sarcasm and cruel imitations of the boss or indiscretions at the copy machine may get easy laughs, but they aren't actually funny. It takes great wisdom to know the right times for and appropriate amounts of humor. All relationships must endure certain amounts of pain and suffering that laughter won't dispel. Yet many tense times can be alleviated with a soft touch of cheer.

Do you know what you get when you cross a termite with a praying mantis? An insect that says grace before eating your house.

You think you can do better than that? Good! Go do it.

INGENUITY OF STEEL

Work on your strengths each day. Your abilities can weaken, and so will your fame. Try to renew your valor, ingenuity, and success daily. Show a new side of your talents daily—displayed fresh like the sun each morning.

When you commit to a rigid program of diet and exercise, others will notice. Excess weight begins to drop off. Muscles begin to tone. Clothes look better on you. Energy and enthusiasm increase. The improvements may be quite significant.

This degree of change isn't quick or easy. It requires much from you—commitment, discipline, sacrifice, and perseverance. Yet the longer you maintain the regimen, the easier it becomes.

Many people pressure us to eat better, exercise, and take care of ourselves physically. All of this is best when backed by a prescription in virtue as well. Just as a regular physical workout is good for the heart and muscles, a daily spiritual workout strengthens the inner qualities of a man or woman.

The secret of success is the same. We must commit to following through with the program. We must practice over and over, every day—even when we don't feel like it. Even when we're tired. Even when we'd rather sink into the sofa, remote in hand.

Physically, a healthy body is important. Improved looks are merely a by-product. For some the goal may be a washboard stomach, buns of steel, or impressive biceps. However, after those things decline (which they will), other benefits of exercise are longer life span and better quality of life.

Even more important is spiritual "centeredness." The commitment and dedication invested in becoming a Godly person are never wasted. The immediate improvements in action and attitude are minor compared to the long-term benefits.

So what do you want to work on today: valor, integrity, humility? Choose one and get started. Your friends will notice the improvement in no time.

NICE GUYS' REPUTATIONS LAST

Prevent scandal. If one bad report spreads, it can blot out your reputation and give you a nickname that is disreputable. Private envy can later turn into broad distrust. It will be easy for others to believe evil about you and hard to dispel the same lie.

This book suggests that the best way to deal with scandal is by living an open and upright life. In this case, however, the focus is on preventing scandal— heading it off at the pass. There are times when the problem is not your behavior but someone else's.

Most of the time we need to deafen ourselves to the undeserved criticism of others. Successful people ignore unfounded complaints and keep working toward their goals. Yet when private envy is the motivation and the complaints turn into various forms of scandal that threaten your reputation, it's time to act.

The best defense for an innocent person is truth. Challenge your critic openly. No doubt his or her strategy involves hit-and-run guerrilla tactics. Rumors and gossip can destroy you when direct accusations never will. As rumors spread, your silence may indicate consent. You need not make a scene or become overly agitated. But if you will have a public face-to-face encounter with your gossipmonger du jour, others will see you have nothing to hide. In open court, you will win.

Celebrities face this type of attack from the tabloids on a regular basis. They know that suing is usually more trouble and expensive than it is worth. Yet when a paper or TV show goes too far with rumor and innuendo, a fat lawsuit usually brings a quick retraction and financial settlement.

It's possible to be a nice person and to be direct with your opponents. Nice people put an end to vicious rumors—and they make their good reputations last a long, long time.

KNOW WHEN TO SAY NO

Know yourself. You cannot master yourself unless you understand your abilities, judgment, and preferences. Study your intellectual abilities for business affairs, and test your courage to apply what you possess. Keep your foundations firm and your head clear for every good work.

It's amazing how much people allow others to determine what they do with their time. Maybe you're being barraged by some of the same people:

> "You've got to read *War and Peace* this summer. It changed my life."

> "Here's the new twelve-volume motivational video series. Watch it and tell me what you think."

> "You need to junk those jazz CDs and start listening to classical—real music."

Don't you know what you like? Then why let someone else tell you!? There's nothing wrong with Tolstoy, motivational videos, or classical music. But if your time is limited and you want to develop yourself, you need to first do what speaks to you. Later, if you have time and energy left, you can check out some leads other people have given you.

Some people only want to go to movies that have been given four-star ratings. They only want to read the books on the *New York Times* best-seller list or those recommended by Oprah. But why not stroll through a bookstore and skim through a few titles to see if anything else looks worthwhile? What appeals to you may not do much for anyone else. We want to think we are so vastly distinct from other people, yet we tend to conform to the "groupthink" mentality of our culture.

If we want to truly get to know ourselves, we may need to say no a lot more than we do. There are all sorts of good reasons why people want you to read, see, or do this and that. But your time is limited—and valuable. You must know your abilities, judgment, and preferences. And then you must push aside anything that impedes your own pursuits. A "no thanks" response at an appropriate time can have very positive results.

LOOK UP FOR WISDOM

Wisdom from above should apply to everything. An ounce of wisdom is worth more than a ton of cleverness. Wisdom is the only true way, though it may not always gain applause from others. Nonetheless, it will be approved by the wise.

Have you ever laughed and nodded through a lecture or seminar, only to get home and realize you didn't really learn anything? If so, you witnessed the difference between cleverness and wisdom.

Many speakers are remarkably clever. They use the right jokes, the right slogans, the right charts and graphs, and the right cultural references. Everything they say is informative and entertaining. Yet their comments may have little to do with everyday problems you might be facing.

In general, a speaker may promote optimism, thinking big, and looking to the future. Nothing wrong with that. Yet in reality, you might be the person forced to deal with negative cash flow, downsizing, and the present. The wise course of action is not always the popular one. While the group may prefer the clever "insight" of the public speaker, their future may depend on your unpopular exercise of wisdom.

Cleverness is usually a self-made trait. A somewhat sharp mind combined with a number of various facts—useful or not—can create a clever persona. But cleverness doesn't make a person wise any more than a fresh coat of paint on a ramshackle barn makes it a new one.

We would do well to strive for wisdom from above, as described in the Bible: "The wisdom that comes from heaven is first of all pure; then peace-loving, considerate, submissive, full of mercy and good fruit, impartial and sincere" (James 3:17). Sounds good. So how do we get it? "If any of you lacks wisdom, he should ask God, who gives generously to all without finding fault, and it will be given to him" (James 1:5).

All it takes to replace ineffective, man-made cleverness with far superior wisdom from above is to ask God for help. It's that easy. And that hard.

WHAT DO YOU WANT TO TALK ABOUT?

Do not be a bore. The person obsessed with one activity or topic becomes tiresome. Brevity is attractive and accomplishes more. This is a form of courtesy that overrides abruptness. Good things, when short, are twice as good. The heart of the matter is greater than the details.

Have you ever been at a party where you didn't know many people and were trying to strike up some conversations? You might let another person know your interests: Irish music, spy novels, breeding golden retrievers, cooking authentic Scandinavian food, or surfing. Yet the other person ignores all you've said and says, "I like cars," and then launches into a nonstop lecture on all the upcoming car events, where to get parts, how to rebuild a carburetor, why Chevys are better than Fords, and how to get grease stains off of your pet. Even if you excuse yourself as quickly as possible, when you circle around and see this person again, he is likely to pick up right where he left off.

The dreaded topic might be cars, past surgeries, military experience, dissatisfaction with one's work, politics, or limitless other possibilities. There's nothing wrong with sharing the things that interest us. However, we must beware of becoming human black holes that suck all the life out of potentially interesting people and festive social occasions.

Well said is soon said. We shouldn't feel the need to dwell too long on what we're saying. If the other person has any interest at all, he or she will ask questions and get a healthy conversation going. And the best way to teach someone how to do this is to model it.

If you don't know what to say when meeting new people and tend to ramble out of nervousness, you can take the focus off yourself by putting it on the other person. Pretend you're Barbara Walters and begin an interview. Think of some of the most interesting questions you can. Then, like any good interviewer, take time to truly listen. Soon the other person will be asking you many of the same things. Before you know it, your brevity will lead to a deep and fulfilling conversation. And if you do it right, it is likely to lead to a new friendship as well.

GREATER EXPECTATIONS

The shortest path to greatness is to go along with others. Relationships with the right people work to your good; manners and tastes are shared, good sense and even talent grow. Opposites beautify and create harmony in the world, and by joining extremes a more effective middle road is found.

The Charles Dickens' classic *Great Expectations* has an interesting plot twist. The main character, Pip, has a mysterious benefactor whom he assumes to be a person he considers great. However, the benefactor turns out to be a convict he had helped as a young child. By not reporting the man, Pip established a relationship that eventually led to unexpected rewards.

The moral of Dickens' story is not to aid and abet criminals but to see in our most casual relationships the potential for something surprising. People may be much more important than we realize.

When young, we like to think of ourselves as independent and self-sufficient. We're strong, healthy, and optimistic. Perhaps we're quick to dismiss those who can't keep up and threaten to hold us back. As we sever a relationship here and there, it becomes easier.

Taken to extremes, this tendency can eventually cause us to shut out spouses and children in order to pursue a career or chase some other intensely personal dream.

People are important—not only for their intrinsic value but to help us get where we want to go. Friendships create synergy where the sum of the whole is greater than the sum of the parts. Other people help us in ways we might not expect—as consultants, role models, therapists, financial sponsors, pen pals, cheerleaders, and more. Even those who hold opinions that are polar opposites of our own can challenge us to deeper understanding of our views—and those of others.

Perhaps it's time to put down the matches and stop burning bridges. Instead, pick up some rope and see if you can build one instead. And as others simultaneously reach out to you, you'll soon develop a web of relationships that will take you anywhere you need to go.

KNOW WHEN TO FOLD 'EM

Do not wait until you are a setting sun. Leave things before things leave you. Wisely withdraw from the mere chance of misfortune, so you won't face it as reality. Wise trainers put racehorses out to pasture before they fall on the field.

It's not too hard to detect gambling fever. For some people, the hope of striking it rich with one big gamble becomes an obsession. A role of seven and the stake doubles. A spin of the wheel and it triples. Or play a long shot and get twenty to one. When we see someone's gambling grow from a pastime to a compulsion, we realize how much the victim needs help and counseling before he or she loses house payments, college funds, and other needed money.

However, there are other fevers that people aren't so quick to identify. Perhaps you know a three-hundred-pound guy who still thinks he looks good in a Speedo, a forty-seven-year-old still clinging to her hippie lifestyle, or a relative who keeps hollering, "I DON'T NEED A HEARING AID." Each of these people may have denial fever, bordering on delusion. And if we're honest with ourselves, perhaps we ignore important problems we need to address.

Growth, change, and aging are natural parts of life. It's not so bad for a horse put out to pasture. He has to adapt to a different lifestyle, to be sure, but it's a lot less work after he gets used to it. Similarly, it's much easier for us to grow content with seeing an older face in the mirror than to spend hours of time and thousands of dollars attempting to keep it looking young. Time and gravity win every time, so wise people aren't afraid to move on to a more mature look and demeanor.

Most people respect those who are older and wiser, but they pity those who refuse to age gracefully. The gamble that you're going to be the exception who is stronger and better looking at seventy than at thirty is not a good bet. As Kenny Rogers sang in "The Gambler," we need to know when to hold our cards and know when to fold them. Know when to walk away. Know when to run.

Walk away from foolish attempts to hold on to the past. Run toward the future. Who cares if you're running a little slower than you used to?

WAVE LINKS

Make friends. A friend is a reflection of yourself. There is no greater blessing than a good deed, and the way to gain a friendly response is to perform friendly acts. Seek someone daily who will wish you well and, hopefully, confide in you.

Perhaps the concepts of making friends and doing good deeds sound a bit childish to you. If so, you're right. It is.

In fact, this was the objective of two children in Ohio. One summer day, two ten-year-old boys decided to stand at a busy intersection and wave to as many people as they could. They devised a game to see how many waves they could get in return. They set a goal of 300—which they doubled in only three hours—so they extended their goal to 1,000 for the day. They didn't stop until they had reached the goal, despite an afternoon thunderstorm.

In addition to the waves that were returned, the boys received one obscene gesture and encountered ten vehicles where no one responded. Overall, their rate of success was remarkable.

If we set out to make friends, we may be surprised at how well it works. It didn't cost these two boys anything to be friendly, yet some people even stopped to encourage them and one woman was moved to tears. We have many more resources and opportunities than most ten-year-olds. What keeps us from trying harder than we do? How long does it take to dial the phone or crank out a short, friendly e-mail?

Are we reluctant to reach out to others, fearing what they might think of us? If so, don't you think it's worth enduring a few apathetic people and an occasional obscene response if the effort also initiates 1,000 potential friendships? Friends can add up quickly.

You may not have 365 new friends by this time next year. You may not have 30 by this time next month. But there's nothing to keep you from having 1 new one by this time tomorrow.

LIFE IS AN EXHIBITION, NOT A COMPETITION

When it comes to people, never compete. Every competition potentially damages your reputation. Our rivals will try to outshine us and few of them play fair. Conflict digs up long-buried skeletons, whereas people of goodwill are always at peace.

Problems that arise from competition have been with us since the beginning of humanity. The serpent in the Garden of Eden was in competition with God and convinced Eve to follow him instead. Cain killed Abel when he decided it was easier to knock off his competition than to make his heart right. And throughout history, serious conflicts have arisen because two or more people were in competition for the girl, the gold, or the glory.

Of course, in this day and age we are surrounded by competition. Peers at work compete for raises and promotions. Our kids compete for our time and attention. And the highly organized business of amateur and professional sports treats competition as the ultimate struggle. Many of our proverbs and expressions are sports related and focus on the all-important goal of winning. But once we get locked into the mentality of winners and losers, there are always a lot more of the latter than the former.

If you and your competitor play fair, but he wins, you don't look good. If you play fair, but he cheats to win, you don't feel good about the contest. If he plays fair, but you cheat to win, you don't feel good about yourself. And if you both cheat, that defeats the whole concept of competition.

How much better it is to take yourself out of the running as far as trying to prove anything by competing. You can still work harder than anyone, but you should do so as a model of integrity rather than merely to win the sales contest. You can still go all out on the racquetball court, but you should do it to improve your game rather than to humiliate your opponent.

Whenever David Letterman introduces his Stupid Pet Tricks segment, he always gives an admonition: "This is an exhibition, not a competition. Please, no wagering." In spite of the humor, it's not a bad philosophy for life. If you live life as a competition, you only allow the opportunity for one person to win. But if you do whatever you can to bring out the best in everyone, you *all* become winners.

UNCOMMON COURTESY

Gain a reputation for courtesy. This in itself will make you likable. Politeness is the main ingredient of culture, just as discourtesy arouses opposition. Pride and bad breeding relate to rudeness. Everyone is honored who gives honor.

Repeat the following phrases aloud:

> "Good morning. How are you?"
>
> "Excuse me."
>
> "Thank you."
>
> "Please."

Have you noticed that you don't hear these phrases as much as you used to? Common courtesy is a lot less common these days. The previous comments, accompanied with a smile, take only seconds. Yet they have the power to influence actions, attitudes, business deals, personal relationships, peace of mind, and so much more.

Courtesy is also a tremendous weapon if you want to influence someone else. Perhaps you can recall a political or religious debate where one of the participants refused to allow the other a fair opportunity to speak.

A polite atheist is likely to come across as more warm, loving, and credible than a raging Christian, regardless of what either of them says.

Most people realize that courtesy requires strength. It isn't easy to sit quietly and listen to people expound views contrary to your own. Yet sometimes it's the courteous thing to do—especially if you hope the other person will listen to your opinion.

Unfortunately, for most of us, curtness has replaced courtesy. We have become snippy, short-tempered, and tuned into only our own personal interests. We have little inclination to tolerate others if we don't have to. We cut them off if they offer alternative opinions.

Since courtesy is in such short supply these days, it tends to get noticed. You might want to try it and see how much of a difference it makes. *Please.*

MAKING THE CORRECT CHANGE

Live practically. Opinions and tastes change with the times. Do not be old-fashioned in your ways of thinking, and let your tastes be modern. But this rule doesn't apply to kindness, for goodness is relevant at all times.

This advice may well have been written upon returning from a high-school reunion after twenty-five years or so. Perhaps you know the experience. It's amazing to see how some people have changed with the times and have matured into fascinating individuals. As the one-time cheerleaders gather to do some old cheers, you realize they are now mothers, corporate CEOs, schoolteachers, community leaders—all much more complex people than they used to be.

But others seem stuck in time. Former football players who haven't exercised in fifteen years still act like jocks. People who lost their popular status right after high school try to get it back for a few hours. Lonely adults try to recapture the close relationships they had as kids. Many reunions can create sadness for the casual observer.

It is the people who are flexible and willing to change who seem to weather the storms of life better.

Driving toward a goal in the future is always better than clinging to an event or accomplishment in the past. We certainly want to carry with us the best of our past—the optimism, the kindness and love, and the tender innocence of youth, but we want to build on those good things rather than hold to them so tightly that they wither and die.

Times change. Attitudes change. Culture changes. Consequently, wise people will change. The Whig party was prominent for about twenty years, but you don't see a lot of Whigs at modern political conventions. As the Whigs disappeared, the Republican party came to light.

Take a good look at your own life—your attitudes, commitments, relationships, thoughts, and priorities. Is it time for a change?

THE CASE FOR GRACE

Grace should season all you do. Grace is revealed even in our thoughts. It is more a natural gift than a product of education and even surpasses good training. It is a shortcut to accomplishment and an escape from embarrassment.

Grace. Mercy. Forgiveness.

We toss these words around as if they are essentially the same things. Worse yet, many of us speak the words, or leave them to the Church, and don't make much of an effort to integrate them into our personal lives. We're usually more familiar with words like justice, revenge, retribution.

In 1987, a Connecticut pastor's son was shot and killed by another man. When the killer was sentenced to five years in prison, the pastor complained that the judgment was not severe enough. But after the killer publicly apologized, the pastor had a change of heart. That's forgiveness. The pastor began to correspond with the killer and even appealed to have his sentence reduced. That's mercy. The killer was released in 1991 and wanted to get married in 1994. He asked the pastor to perform the ceremony, which he did. That's grace. The pastor eventually gave the other man his love, acceptance, and a new start at life—things that many of us might not think the man deserved.

Sometimes we try to practice grace without actually feeling gracious. We act civilly toward someone, yet in our minds are scenes of what we really would like to see happen to the offending person. Some of us have probably also blasted someone for an offense, only to find out too late that we were accusing the wrong person.

True grace should begin in our hearts and flow out through our actions. We can avoid much embarrassment that way. Our willingness to show grace is even likely to become a secret of our success. When grace becomes genuine and frequent, it can be truly amazing.

ANGERS AWAY

There is an art in leaving things alone. There are hurricanes in human affairs, tempests of passion, when it is wise to retire to a harbor and ride it out with the anchor in place. To yield now is to conquer later. Let disturbance run its course.

A new phrase is making its way into our language: "road rage." This term refers to the excessive anger some people display during highway commutes. As the roads get more congested, the drivers' irritation levels soar—patience plummets. Wise people are reluctant to use their horns for any reason, lest another driver take offense and literally start a fight. The best thing to do is sit quietly until traffic is moving again and then try to get around the guy doing only twenty-seven miles per hour in the passing lane (because he's so involved in a cell phone conversation).

Yet if we were more honest with ourselves, we might identify other related maladies: spouse rage, teenage-child rage, work rage, or any number of other possibilities. In each case, it may be that the best course of action is inaction.

Just as we can't control the weather, we have little say about the storms of life we encounter. Some become all-out hurricanes. All of our huffing and puffing pales in contrast to their effect. The best we can do is to ride it out. Batten down the hatches. Board up the windows. Retreat to the most secure place we know.

No storm will last forever. When the winds die down and the sun shines again, then we can restore communication and try to make ourselves heard. In doing so, we don't yield the victory; we merely postpone it. Proper timing is every bit as important as proper action.

The next time you see a big storm brewing, don't add your own fury to the rage that already exists. Try dropping your anchor instead. See if your anger doesn't drop as well.

TOMORROW IS ANOTHER DAY

Recognize bad days, times when nothing goes well. To turn out well, a particular activity must be done on the right day. Take hold of the opportunity—don't throw away the least chance. Yet don't judge anything on a single day's good or bad fortune.

You won't find a much better experience than a picnic on a perfect, sunny day. Yet if you insist on having that picnic when there's an 85 percent probability of thundershowers, you might regret it—especially if you pack the kids and the dogs into the minivan, drive an hour to the park, and get everything unloaded just seconds before the clouds burst. You run the risk of getting everything soaking wet, having the kids catch cold, and having to remove the seats in your minivan to clean all the muddy-dog paw prints. Waiting a day can make life a lot more convenient and fun.

Or if you're feeling sick while preparing a presentation, will your boss and coworkers understand your presentation? Will it be your best work? Like an attorney who is not quite ready to represent his client, there are days we need to seek a continuance in order to perform at our best. Waiting a day can help us do our best work and make a better impression on others.

Also wise is to refrain from making big decisions based on one day's experience. Sometimes an occasional fisherman will buy himself a boat after one exceptional day out with a friend—then never use it enough for his investment to pay off. (The same goes for Salad Shooters, convertibles, bread makers, and thousands of other products.) Waiting a day to make purchasing decisions can save a lot of money.

Planes won't take off when it's too foggy. Similarly, people who live in the north soon learn not to make life decisions in February. The long winters can affect moods and opinions. It's much better to wait until the "fog" lifts and one's brain has the benefit of warmth and sunshine.

There's a time for everything. The time for decision just might be tomorrow.

HEAR, HEAR

Seek out the advice of others. He is an unteachable donkey who will not listen to anyone. Even the powerful and independent must learn to lean on others. A friend must be free to advise you, even to criticize, without feeling threatened. Our trust in him should give him that power.

Most of us want the advice of others. The problem is, we want the other person's advice to confirm what we've already decided to do. As long as the other opinion enforces ours, everything is hunky-dory. It's when the other person strongly opposes us that we tend to become sanctimonious.

Perhaps if we would learn to ask for advice earlier in the decision-making process, we would get better results. Too often we plod ahead in ambition and ignorance, doing the best we can on our own, which may not be as good as we had hoped. If we wait until that point to ask, "What do you think?" we shouldn't be offended if another person honestly replies, "Eh, not so great." It is during the planning stage that we need to seek out good counselors. If we ask, "What do you think?" early in the process, we can implement the good and honest responses we receive.

Why should we make our friends suffer if we're the ones who are stubborn (donkey-like)? True friends want the best for us and will be honest, even when we'd rather have a sugarcoated response. We should not only be willing to listen, but we should have a genuine respect for their honesty.

The comparison to a donkey is a good one. Donkeys have large ears yet don't seem to hear instructions very well. When it comes to good advice, how well do your ears work?

CONVERSATION PEACE

Learn the art of conversation. This is where your full personality can emerge. Though this is a common event, no act requires more attention. Every conversation is a loss or gain to you. The wise sense the pulse of your soul, and your intelligence is displayed. Discretion is more important than sounding profound.

Con•ver•sa•tion \ n : oral exchange of sentiments, observations, opinions, or ideas

That's how Webster defines it. But to be honest, sometimes our definition may be closer to, "What happens when I open my mouth and start rambling, while other people sit and listen." We frequently neglect the exchange portion of Webster's definition. "Lecture" and "conversation" are two very different things.

Conversation style is closely related to personality. A self-centered person can usually be identified after a short conversation. So can a kind and giving person. So can a timid person. Or a bully, a gossip, a con man, and so forth.

However, we can learn the art of conversation. A shy person need not blend into the wallpaper at every gathering. All it takes is a little practice. A few well-chosen questions, a couple of appropriate comments about one's own interests, a little time to let the other person think and reply, and before you know it a conversation is taking place—a truly genuine and interesting conversation. Similarly, a blowhard can learn to converse by closing his mouth long enough to let others speak. Who knows, he might even learn something!

We would do well to approach every conversation with the eagerness of drilling for oil. Sometimes we hit dry holes. Sometimes we hit a gusher. But occasionally we discover deep and valuable resources that are to be treasured.

Talk is cheap. Good conversation, on the other hand, is priceless.

A PASSION FOR PRUDENCE

Learn the art of mastering your passions. Stand against the rude advances of passion by first using prudent reflection. Gain command over your temper, not going beyond a certain point. Every excess is a departure from rational conduct. No one is wise when he is already on horseback.

General George Patton was a brilliant military strategist. He accomplished things others thought impossible. Yet one day he slapped a shell-shocked soldier who was afraid to return to battle. His action received a lot of negative press. Consequently, his career path seemed to plateau as officers with lesser records were promoted above him. If Patton had gained command over his temper to the extent he commanded his men, he might have done much better for himself.

King David was a man after God's own heart. A nine-foot giant couldn't stop him. Saul's entire army couldn't capture him. Hoards of hostile Philistines couldn't defeat him. But when he spied one woman bathing on a rooftop, his inner lusts took over and his life began to crumble.

Anger. Lust. Coveting. Power. Money. Any of these passions can topple us if we allow them to overpower our common sense. It's a difficult balance to feel passionately about certain things without allowing our passions to run amok and create trouble. If we wish to load up one side of the scale with intense passions, we must counterbalance the other side with prudence and control. Think of passion as a strong and somewhat wild horse, eager to run with speed and power. Prudence is the bit in his mouth that provides direction and control. Without the bit, the horse will run where he wants. But with it, you can win races.

And speaking of horses, we need to have a wise plan before we jump up on horseback and go riding off. Perhaps we would do well to get down off our horses for a while, especially if they're high ones.

ALL IS NOT FAIR IN LOVE AND WAR

You may have to wage war against something, but don't use poisoned arrows. A crooked victory brings no glory with it but instead brings disgrace. The slightest treachery hurts your good name. If gallantry, generosity, and faith are lost, you should be the one to recover them.

As weapons were developed and nations continued to go to war against each other, wise people began to see the need for some basic rules for both sides to abide by. Chemical or germ warfare, for example, is an atrocious concept for most soldiers. The threat of death or injury is enough in itself without using science to see how vile or nasty we can make the death. Even war has rules.

How about your personal conflicts? Do you play fair, or do you change the rules to fit your moods? Do you expect to be treated fairly by others yet resort to sneak attacks when nothing else works for you? Many of us have a rather shifty personal strategy for dealing with others. Perhaps we even achieve victory. But if it's a crooked victory, we can take little joy in it.

It doesn't matter whether you're talking about war or professional wrestling, people are going to rally around the side that is more fair. As soon as one of the participants is caught cheating, public opinion usually swings strongly toward the one who has been taken advantage of.

Dueling seems like a barbaric way to solve problems, but at least it was out in the open. The people engaged in conflict used the same weapons and had witnesses to ensure that the rules were properly carried out. On a level playing field with equal armament, at least both parties had a chance to win. A strategy of deceit, lies, or similar poisoned arrows is even more barbaric than stepping off ten paces, turning, and shooting.

We can do more than just fight fair. Even in our conflicts we are to bring a sense of gallantry, generosity, and faith. But then, if we really tried to bring these characteristics to our disagreements, we might discover little to fight about.

IN CASE OF EMERGENCY

Do not waste favors from others. If you use up great favors for small results, what is there later for the big needs? Nothing is more valuable than a protector, and nothing costs more nowadays than a favor. It is more important to have these people's support than many possessions.

Suppose you're celebrating a birthday in a hotel restaurant. When the cake comes, you have a bit of trouble blowing out all those candles, so you go down the hallway, smash the glass, get a fire extinguisher, and return to your table to finish the job. What do you think the other party goers would think of your behavior?

Depending on how you normally behave, such an action might not seem strange at all. But for most people, this would be very eccentric behavior, bordering on all-out weird. Most people realize that fire extinguishers are available in case of emergency, and a birthday cake simply doesn't qualify.

We would be wise to take a similar approach to calling in favors. Rather than doing so indiscriminately, perhaps we should save them in case of emergency. If a friend calls at 3:00 A.M. to explain that his car won't start and he needs your help to get his pregnant wife to the hospital right away, he is going to feel an obligation after you help him out. You then have the option of dangling your good deed in front of him and making his life miserable: "I don't care if the Super Bowl is on. I'm in the mood for a Big Mac. You owe me a favor, buddy. Get going!" But you also have the option of downplaying the favor, while keeping the person's name in mind in case of emergency. In the event of a future crisis, it's comforting to know that you have a person or two to call on who wouldn't mind being inconvenienced for a genuine need.

If more of us learn to infuse wisdom into our daily lives, perhaps we won't face quite as many emergencies.

AVOIDING THOSE CLOSE SHAVES

Never show your enemy what he should do. Fools never do what the wise expect of them, for they don't have discretion. The wise person follows a hidden path, looking at matters from both angles. Think about all that could happen rather than what will happen.

"Never show your enemy what he should do." This is another of those pieces of advice that seems so obvious it need not even be committed to paper. Yet the assumption is even more vital: Know who your enemies are.

Don't forget the story of Samson. His strength was sufficient for him to take on a thousand enemies at a time. No problem. But then his enemies got smart and bribed his girlfriend to discover the secret of his strength. He made up three different stories, and each time the Philistines leaped out of the shadows to subdue him. You'd think the big lug would have figured out he was being set up. It may not be that he was so much blinded by love, because the Bible describes Delilah's strategy: "With such nagging she prodded him day after day until he was tired to death" (Judges 16:16). Samson finally told her the truth and soon thereafter met his defeat. Delilah was his enemy, and he told her exactly what she should do.

Few of us are so dense that we expose our weak points to known enemies. But some of us, like Samson, get confused as to who our enemies really are. Perhaps it is while trying to win a friend or build a relationship that we reveal more about ourselves than is wise. We envision the best thing that could happen by becoming intimate and vulnerable, when in actuality many less positive things are just as likely to occur.

Wise people follow a hidden path—they keep their mouths shut much of the time. They don't announce every strategy prior to enacting it. And they certainly don't make it easy for their enemies to strategize against them.

During World War II, billboards reminded people that "Loose lips sink ships." Loose lips are just as dangerous today, but it might be your career, your relationships, or your reputation in danger. A little wisdom—and a little silence—can avoid many such sinking feelings.

THE PRAISE CHASE

Praise what is proper. This will show your taste rests on excellent things and that you value them before others. Praise gives us topics to discuss and encourages worthwhile endeavors. Others admire mediocrity and speak poorly of everyone else. Don't be dismayed by flattery or criticism.

"Mr. Hart, here's a dime. Call your mother. Tell her there's serious doubt about your becoming a lawyer."

This classic line from the movie, *The Paper Chase,* is spoken by the John Houseman character, Professor Kingsfield. He was laconic, emotionless, and merciless to those who needed affirmation. Student Jonathan Hart almost gave up on law school because of him. Yet Kingsfield's expertise and reputation were impeccable, so Mr. Hart was determined to impress him. Kingsfield never offered a word of praise, yet the viewer sees him mark a large bold A on Hart's final exam—the most emphatic praise possible. If Mr. Hart hadn't been truly excellent, he never would have made the grade.

The Professor Kingsfields of the world are frustrating. We want so desperately to impress them—and to know we have done so—yet it is next to impossible to receive a word of praise. Contrast this tendency with people who are so free with their praise that it means absolutely nothing. Every single thing you do is great or wonderful. Which would you prefer: a once-in-a-blue-moon acknowledgment of truly excellent work or gushing praise over performances you clearly know were mediocre?

Most of us agree that excessive praise is worthless praise. Even young children figure this out. A parent who puts every single test and piece of artwork on the refrigerator doesn't do the child any favors. The kid realizes he doesn't even need to try. Wise parents praise what is proper. When a child tries very hard and then receives appropriate praise, he or she feels properly rewarded and motivated.

When you praise someone, is it genuine and direct? Does the other person feel warm and adequately rewarded? Or does she feel like it's just one more worthless comment to stick on her fridge?

THE CONSOLATION PRIZE

Find consolation in all things. Even trouble has its consolation. Be frugal and you will live long. Those people who matter most will be in short supply, and the people who are good for nothing will be everywhere. Yet there is no cloud without a silver lining.

Did you ever win a consolation prize? Perhaps as a child you entered a contest and were just one point short of winning the grand prize—a shiny chrome bicycle with a cool banana seat and tassel streamers on the handlebars. But since you worked so hard and got so close, they gave you a consolation prize— perhaps a plastic egg containing Silly Putty.

The natural tendency was to focus on what you missed out on. You kept kicking yourself for not winning the bicycle. True, the prize you received didn't seem like much next to the one you missed. But if you only could have focused on what you did receive, you might have done a lot better. After all, you didn't have Silly Putty that morning, but after the contest you did. That night you could have had all kinds of new fun: bouncing it like a ball, reproducing your favorite comic-strip characters and stretching them out, getting it stuck in your sister's hair, etc.

As we get older, we miss out on more and more things. And, regretfully, people stop handing out consolation prizes. As mature adults, we must find our own consolation in the disappointing or tragic events of life. Yet if we look hard enough, we can almost always find the silver lining. A devastating breakup can lead to a new love interest who becomes a spouse of fifty years. A horrible job interview can shut one door yet provide an unexpected opportunity with more fulfilling employment. In such cases, the consolation turns out to be better than the grand prize. In other instances the consolation isn't as satisfying, but at least it's something.

You're not a kid anymore. Don't expect a lot of consolation prizes. From now on, try to see consolation as the prize.

REVEALING HIDDEN MOTIVES

Watch out for people who begin with someone else's concern and end with their own. Be watchful for their intentions. Unless you understand their motives, you may be forced to take their chestnuts out of the fire and then damage your own fingers. Many make others serve them, so quickly learn from their motives.

The phone rings when you're in the middle of dinner. What do you know? Someone offers you an all-expense-paid trip to Hawaii, mumbling something about a time-share. What luck! It rings again an hour later, in the middle of your favorite show, and you discover you're the lucky winner of some free magazine subscriptions. A half-hour later, in the midst of a thrilling game of Candyland with your kids, another caller lets you know you're preapproved to receive a credit card. What an incredibly fortunate night this has been for you!

Unfortunately, this type of night is all too average for most of us. Telemarketers call incessantly with all kinds of "free" offers and opportunities. To hear them talk, they're doing you a huge favor because you're such a special person—every bit as special as the other thousands of people on their lists.

Most of us try to keep up with the latest schemes and scams of people trying to sell their products under the guise of doing us a favor. We know their ultimate goal is for their company to line its pockets with our hard-earned cash.

So why aren't we a bit more street-smart when it comes to interpersonal relationships? Close associates may be just as willing to take advantage of us if we allow it. They would never say so, of course. They always have a good sales pitch to get our attention and support.

In many cases, when pressure or trouble arises, they're looking out for number one, and you're the one who gets burned trying to save their chestnuts.

SHOW ME THE MERIT!

Find your success by merit, not by presumption.
Respect comes through merit, and diligence makes the
path shorter. Integrity is not enough, and being
overbearing is degrading. The middle road between
deserving and advocating should be pursued as you go
up the ladder.

Jerry Maguire was an academy-award-nominated
movie that cleverly critiqued the problems and
challenges of sports agents. The most quoted line from
the movie was, "Show me the money!" which was the
demand of Maguire's only client. Yet both athlete and
agent discovered the frustration of playing for money
rather than for merit and respect. When both
rediscovered the genuine love for what they were
doing, they also found the satisfaction that had been
eluding them.

It seems that athletes these days are never more
prominent in the news than when signing new multi-
million-dollar contracts. Such events are based on
presumption—what the athlete is supposed to do in the
future. Certainly he or she has shown promise in the
past, yet the cumulative merit of past accomplishments

never seems to garner the same attention as a fat contract. Few athletes manage to live up to the expectations placed on them from such a high advance. Someone shows them the money, but too often they are never shown the respect they crave.

Our lives should be lived on a get-paid-as-you-go basis. We need to focus on merit. The things we do each and every day should amount to something. Even though we may get paychecks, benefits, and bonuses whether or not we excel, contentment comes from the merit of the work rather than the presumption of reward.

Some people evaluate success based on the size of the salary. Most who do then wonder why they feel so unfulfilled. If you dare to show your boss, your family, and your friends the merit of a diligent life without being overbearing, you won't have to ask them to show you their love and respect.

THE CREAM OF THE CROP

Know the great people of your age, for there are few. There is usually one great leader in each field. Yet mediocrity is as widespread as foolishness. Many claim the title "Great," in vain, for without great deeds, the title means nothing.

Here's a little quiz to see how up to date you are on current events.

> Who won the Heisman trophy last year?
>
> Who was voted MVP in the NBA?
>
> Who is the current reigning Miss America?
>
> Who took home the Grammies for best male and female pop vocalist?
>
> Who last received the Nobel prize for peace? Economics? Chemistry?
>
> Who received the most recent Pulitzer prizes?
>
> Who is secretary of the treasury? Secretary of the interior?
>
> During the past five years, what people have become prominent in the fields of opera, religion, physics, jazz music, and education?

Keeping up with the "great people of our age" is difficult for a number of reasons. For one, we tend to segment our interests to maximize our free time and/or remain authoritative in our chosen area(s) of interest. Sports fans may be quite limited when it comes to knowing music groups or academic leaders, just as music groupies might have trouble quoting batting averages or shooting percentages.

Another problem is that our culture determines what is important. People make a big deal about movies and beauty contests, yet we rarely see a big production number to celebrate the discovery of a new quark or the nomination of a new cabinet member. Famous sports figures and musicians are frequent lead stories, but we have to wait until further into the newscast to hear about some of the more significant people.

Finally, we hear numerous acclaims that are self-described rather than time-tested. Aretha Franklin has earned her "Queen of Soul" designation, but many other titles and nicknames come closer to shameless self-promotion than truth in advertising.

They say cream rises to the top. It's too bad we so often pay no mind to the rich and nutritious cream of the crop and remain satisfied with skim milk.

BOOR JUDGMENT

There are rude and boorish people everywhere. But vulgar opposition can be worse. Highborn people without manners are great disciples of ignorance and avid for degrading gossip. Don't notice what these people say, still less what they think.

Why be polite and mannerly when we know it's rude and boorish behavior that grabs headlines, sells books, packs comedy clubs, and promotes records? Why watch a talk show where someone is engaged in informative and polite conversation when you can change channels and see Roseanne's latest tattoo, Dennis Rodman in a dress, or Jerry Springer's tasteless topic of the day?

Yet who can blame celebrities for going over the top in terms of behavior? In most cases, they're only giving people what they want. If the celebrity's behavior didn't boost ratings or sell products, most of them wouldn't bother. Frankly, they don't have to work very hard to get laughs and attention. The use of a certain word or two, or the mention of a particular body part or function, and the crowd starts whooping it up. If we don't make them exert much effort to impress us, is that their fault or ours?

Therefore, it's more or less up to us as to what we will support. We need not join organized boycotts or protest groups. We just need to stop spending our money on "vulgar" products and quit watching tasteless programs. In many cases, the slightest decline in sales or popularity makes more of a difference than most people realize. When the money and/or attention dries up, so will the outrageous behavior. (By the way, have you ever noticed how many people known for vulgar humor or skin flicks quickly try to shed their reputation when given an opportunity to be perceived as a serious actor or comedian?)

Every time you're faced with rude and boorish people—whether in the media or in real life—you are a judge. For famous personalities, you can deem them to be worth watching and add to their ratings. Or you can use your remote control to change channels and execute the "death penalty" in the form of low ratings and cancellation.

Of course, in real life it's even easier to pass judgment on rude people. You can just turn around and walk the other way.

WHEN TWO HEADS AREN'T BETTER

Never act from stubbornness but from wisdom. Obstinacy is a sickness of the mind, an offspring of passion that is never right. There are people who don't know how to get along in peace. They want to do everything through cunning, but their judgment is damaged and so are their hearts.

Strange things begin to happen when groups of people assemble and try to work together, be it juries, church committees, or corporate work teams. Almost immediately, control-oriented people try to put themselves in charge. The more of these people in the group, the harder it is to get geared up and going. Others don't necessarily want to lead, but they want to be heard. No matter how many people are participating, these people feel the need to state their opinions on each and every minute point.

But one of the most interesting and most damaging behaviors is when two or more people become completely at odds with one another. They cease to care whether or not they win or lose an argument. The goal becomes simply to make sure the other person doesn't win. If this happens, progress and productivity essentially come to a halt. When stubbornness and obstinacy take over, the issues of right and wrong become insignificant. It doesn't matter what one person says, the other is against it!

The trouble is, people who get caught up in this confrontational mentality are easy targets for wise opponents. If you establish a reputation for never agreeing with your enemies, they soon learn to manipulate your decisions. All they have to do is state the opinion opposite theirs. By opposing them, you will actually argue their point for them after which they can admit defeat and do things your way (which is actually what they wanted all along). You win the argument only by losing the war. Of course, you've already lost sight of reality, so additional losses are to be expected.

Opposing opinions, when discussed openly and honestly, can lead to surprising new revelations and perhaps some middle ground that satisfies everyone involved. But there is no place for stubbornness and obstinacy in the process. Having everyone else do things your way might be nice. But having everyone (including yourself) do things the right way is even better.

A CLOTHES CALL

If you cannot clothe yourself as a lion, then clothe yourself as a fox. Use cleverness when force will not do. Take either way, the king's highway of courage or the path of cunning. Skill has accomplished more than force, and strategy has conquered courage more often than not.

Perhaps you put a lot of time and thought into looking good. When you have an important meeting or appointment, you want to get just the right blouse and skirt combination or select a tie that will show you are bold without being overly flashy. Clothes make the person, so they say, and entire volumes have been written about how to dress for success.

Yet we are faced with an even more basic "clothing" decision we need to make. To a large extent, we control our daily demeanor. How we choose to drape the outer person is of little significance compared to our fundamental inner mentality.

Some days we need to appear a bit more ferocious than normal. When confronted with hard times, aggressive enemies, or other threats, it is frequently better to bite back than to merely bow under the pressure. Regardless of our normal personalities, sometimes we need a roaring good "lion" day.

On other days our power and courage will be in short supply. So when you can't be a lion, be a fox instead. We should always be able to rely on wit, cunning, and strategy. In fact, those qualities might be more effective on any given day than power or fierceness.

What are you going to wear today? Just remember: It's a zoo out there, so dress accordingly.

THE GREATEST STORY NEVER TOLD

Have an element of the business person. Life should consist of action as well as thought. The extreme focus on higher things leaves no time for things close at hand. The prudent person should be like a good business executive, dealing with the necessary things.

Suppose you're hired as a movie producer. You're completely in charge. You find a well-crafted screenplay, witty and poignant, that is sure to make the audience howl with laughter and weep unashamedly (in all the right places, of course). You hire a casting director who signs up Newman, Redford, Streep, Pacino, Schwarzenegger, and many more big names. You line up the hottest new director. You plan to shoot in Hawaii, New Zealand, and other breathtaking locations. But you don't even get nominated for an Oscar because, uh, you just never got around to making the film.

No matter how much thought a person puts into a project, nothing is accomplished if decisive action isn't taken. Military leaders realize wars can be won or lost, depending on appropriate actions. General George Patton is quoted as saying, "A good plan, violently executed right now, is a lot better than a perfect plan executed next week."

Business people also know how important it is to act. Without action, good people remain unemployed, good products sit in the warehouse rather than getting shipped out, good opportunities disappear as quickly as they come, and good sales projections plummet into huge financial losses. Five-year plans may be important but not as much as what happens today.

Some people put intensive thought into what they want their lives to be—careers, families, accomplishments, development of talents, and so forth. The "script" is strong. The cast is brilliant. The plot is fascinating. But sadly, they never get around to acting on their plans. In such cases, what begins as a fascinating action/adventure almost always turns out to be an uninteresting "sleeper."

ARE YOU UP TO THE ASK?

Know how to ask for things. For some this is very easy; for others it is quite difficult. To ask one who cannot refuse, no skill is required. But don't ask after another has been refused or after a time of sorrow.

It's Christmas morning. You've just opened your gifts, and you're staring in disbelief at the largest, gaudiest ceramic pig you've ever seen in your life. Your little sister, on the other hand, has a crisp new $100 bill. Why? Because when Aunt Edna asked what you wanted for Christmas, your sister was direct and said, "Money!" You, on the other hand, put on your best "aw-shucks" face and said, "I'll be happy with anything you get me, Auntie." So are you happy now?

The line between directness and politeness is a fine one. No one appreciates the person who is always demanding her own way—nor the one who goes into a whining fit to get what she wants. Yet there are numerous opportunities in life to come right out and state your opinions and preferences, asking specifically for what you want. It is at these junctions where the person who knows how to ask for things can flourish. Sometimes directness is the best course of action.

The trick comes in determining which opportunities are appropriate and which aren't. It's not the wisest move to march into the boss's office and ask for a big raise the moment after someone else has tried and has been given the heave-ho. When a grandfather dies, it's tacky (and foolish) to interrupt your grandmother's mourning process to be clear with her about which of his possessions you wish to inherit. Street-smart people develop a clear sense of timing as well as the courage to ask for what they want.

What do you want? Directions? A promotion? Someone to go to dinner with? The key to the restroom? By all means, learn to ask for these things. Whether or not your request is granted, you'll feel better simply for asking. If you don't learn the art of asking, spend that time cleaning out your closets instead. You'll need lots of room to store the ceramic pigs and similar souvenirs you're bound to accumulate throughout your lifetime.

DONE YET?

Push yourself. Some put all their strength into beginning a project and never finish it. They invent ideas but never execute them. For some it is due to impatience, for others it is a lack of contentment with the result. These people are either incapable or unreliable. If the undertaking is good, why not finish it?

Started any good undertakings lately? More importantly, have you finished any?

Most people know what would be good for them or what they might enjoy. They go back to school for another degree, take up clarinet lessons, or start remodeling the basement. They know from the start that these activities won't be easy and will require a lot of perseverance, yet high enthusiasm plunges them into the project.

However, it doesn't take long to discover that enthusiasm is a fickle feeling. It can disappear in an instant—usually the instant after the person pays a large nonrefundable deposit for tuition, buys a top-of-the-line clarinet, or rips out the basement walls down to the studs. It is at that point that the hole left by the retreat of enthusiasm must be replaced with something else—commitment, willpower, and stubborn dedication. Only by following through will the project come to a beneficial end. Otherwise, the person is not only left with an expensive mess, he or she comes across looking foolish as well.

Impatience and discontentment are our enemies but not insurmountable ones. Both can be defeated with mild, but consistent, levels of persistence. This is not to say that it's always bad to walk away from things. Many people find great satisfaction in trying lots of different things to see which they like and which they don't. But after determining what should be pursued, we need to make sure a little laziness or fear doesn't stand in the way of seeing those things through to successful completions.

Enthusiasm may disappear early in the project. But if you commit to the project and don't give up, enthusiasm will return and bring its friends—hope, joy, and contentment. The feeling of satisfaction is worth all the trouble, but you never can be satisfied with a job well done until the job is, well, done.

A SILENT, BUT ACTIVE, PARTNER

Ignatius Loyola offered this advice, "Use human means as if there were no divine ones and divine means as if there were no human ones."

In business, partners depend on each other. They both bring skills and energy to the partnership. When one person makes a big sale or comes up with a great idea, the other is as thrilled as if it had been himself. Many partners work quite independently of each other yet get excited when they meet and see what the other has been doing.

Loyola suggests a similar approach to life with God as a partner. With the challenges and possibilities of life laid out before us, we cannot afford to twiddle our thumbs and wait for heavenly signs before taking action. We are gifted with unique skills and insights, and we need to put them to good use.

At the same time, we realize that our Partner is doing the lion's share of the work, often unseen and unnoticed. We must count on His help, especially for the things over which we have no control or influence. In many cases, the best thing we can possibly do is sit back and let Him handle things. But we should never sit on our hands. Those we should keep busy doing the things we can do.

If a loved one gets cancer, leave it to God to provide the peace, courage, and strength needed. You, on the other hand, can provide companionship, soup, and faithful devotion. You can do all you know to do. God will do His part.

One more thing about a business partnership: Both partners reap the rewards and payoffs. The positive things you do bring glory to God. Similarly, you reap the benefits of His gifts: His presence, personal concern, love, peace, forgiveness, and more. If you tend to complain about how much is expected of you, think about the involvement of both partners. Then decide who's getting the better deal.

THANKS, BUT I DON'T NEED TO KNOW

Do not explain yourself too much. Most people do not value what is plain but admire what they don't fully comprehend. You should appear wiser than is required in order to be held in high opinion. Give them no time to criticize; they should spend time trying to comprehend your full meaning.

Did you ever ask someone for directions and get way more information than you needed to know? "Well, you go down this street a ways, past the Red Roof Inn, the interstate overpass, and the Ford car dealership—until you get to an intersection with a Shell station, a pancake house, an art gallery, and a pet store. Turn left and go until you see a Mobil station on the left and a Citgo on the right. But go straight until you find a 7-Eleven. Not the first one you come to, though. It's the third one, I think. Turn right and you'll cross a bridge and a railroad track. If you get to the Gulf station, you've gone too far and you'll need to turn around and go back to the Burger King. Now you're about halfway there . . ."

You begin to wonder why they call them directions. Don't you much prefer to have a person say, "The place you're looking for is six blocks west and two blocks north"? That's all the information you need.

It's a joy to converse with people who make appropriate comments and then stop talking. Some people seem to think they're getting paid by the word. Others, to cover an embarrassing shortage of knowledge on the current topic, go off on numerous tangents. But all they are doing is creating a lot of confusion.

How much better it is to state the facts as you know them, add your opinions if you wish, and then allow others to do the same. This may appear to be a bold new method of communication to some people. It may even seem to them that you're something of a simpleton at first, but don't worry. It puts them in the position of doing the same thing, and then you get to see how much they really know. It's amusing to see how, when you stick to the topic and give them all a chance to talk, many of them suddenly have nothing to say.

GIVE 'TIL IT DOESN'T HURT

Do good a little at a time but often. With many people it is not necessary to overburden them with favors or you will lose them altogether. They cannot repay you and would prefer to be enemies rather than debtors. Give what costs you little yet is much desired and appreciated all the more.

It's becoming more difficult to get excited about voluntary giving. Each year it seems that additional days are designated that require giving: Secretary's Day, Grandparents' Day, Sweetest Day, and so forth. Each day the mail brings pleas from numerous organizations with tragic stories and self-addressed reply envelopes. Each Christmas it gets a bit harder to decide whom to buy gifts for and how much to spend.

By the time we give when we must, pay back the gifts we have received, and try to give enough to non-profit groups to keep from feeling guilty, it's difficult to feel good about giving. The institution of giving has essentially taken all the fun out of it.

We can scale way, way back and still make people happy if we're just a bit more frequent with our giving. Rather than a once-a-year gift exchange that maxes out credit-card limits and creates the stress of hoping the other person will like it, why not simplify? An unexpected card can do wonders to pick up someone's spirits. A tin of cookies works even better. An invitation to dinner. A five-minute chat on the front porch. Bakery pastry for coffee break—for no special reason. These types of gifts are essentially stress free, and you can do a lot of this kind of giving for the cost of a dozen roses and a box of candy. You can affect more people. You can actually have fun.

Presents are expected at Christmas and on birthdays. But when someone gets something nice when he or she isn't expecting it, now that's a gift. You'll feel great by doing it and even better when others catch on and return the favors.

The secret to successful giving is not finding the one great "gift that keeps on giving." It is far preferable to become a giver who keeps on giving.

FORGET ABOUT IT!

Be able to forget. The things we remember best are often those that are best forgotten. Memory is active in the painful things but often neglects to remember pleasures. Often, the only remedy for trouble is to forget it. Nevertheless, good habits of memory can improve one's quality of life.

Suppose you do a small favor for someone who greatly appreciates it. He or she might say, "I owe you one." Your reply is likely to be, "Forget about it!"

Suppose someone does something that causes you pain, sorrow, or embarrassment but later apologizes. Perhaps you say, "I forgive you. Let's put this behind us and act as if it never happened."

In both cases, your relationship with the person is likely to depend on your ability to forget. If you can't create some spontaneous amnesia, the relationships will become strained. You don't want to greet friends while secretly thinking, *This guy still owes me a favor—no, two favors!* And you don't want to go through life recalling past grievances each time you run into the offending party. Before you know it, every time you meet someone your pesky memory will dredge up negative thoughts.

To avoid such problems, consider good habits of memory. As you think about people—your enemies as well as your friends—a really good memory is able to go far enough back to recall positive things. If memory only goes back to the latest conflict, it's not a very good one. Most people have decent qualities that more than compensate for their faults. A good memory will recall all the person's qualities, and you can then focus on the more pleasant ones.

It's your choice. You can go through life remembering things that tick you off, but that option does neither you nor the other person(s) any good. Or you can work a bit harder to recall special times and shared events that have brought you closer together. A vast difference in outlook and outcome lies in whether or not your memory serves you well.

NO LAX OF EFFORT

Try to avoid a careless day. Fate may catch us unaware and play tricks on us. Our intelligence, courage, and other virtues must be prepared for the test. Carefulness fails just when it is most needed. Military strategy puts strengths on trial before battle and when least expected.

Some people suggest that when buying a car, you first determine on what day of the week it was made. The theory is that cars made on Mondays are not as good because workers are coming off the weekend and may not be as astute as they need to be. If they're too sleepy or hung over to notice minor flaws, you may suffer for it. It is also thought that Friday-made cars might have similar defects because workers are gearing up for the next weekend and may be a bit too festive or in a hurry to do their best work.

Getting a lemon of a car is bad enough, but consider the effect of bad days in other vocations. You want to think that surgeons, air-traffic controllers, firefighters, hostage negotiators, and people in similar professions are always at peak performance. If not, the consequences can be devastating for many others beside themselves.

Yet why expect more of such people than we do of ourselves? Certainly, we can't avoid the occasional bad day when things are beyond our control. Yet far too often we tend to say, "I had a bad day," when in reality what we should say is:

> "I was really lazy today and didn't get much done."

> "I lost my temper today and made life miserable for everyone."

> "The boss ignored me today, so I didn't work very hard."

> "I was supposed to return an important phone call today, and I didn't."

Any of these things can create a bad day, yet these are all events over which we have control. It's not that we *had* a bad day; we *made* it a bad day. Try to have a good day—even if it is Monday.

BETTER, SAFE, AND NOT SORRY

In anything you do, if you know only a little, stick to the safe path. What has worked before will work again. Remember that whatever you know, security is safer than being unique.

Yesterday you learned to ski. You found it quite exhilarating to feel the wind racing through your hair as you sped down the bunny slope. To be truthful, you found it thrilling to be able to stand upright without falling on some different and embarrassing part of your body.

Today, however, you're ready for a bigger challenge. You find a new slope labeled "Death Run 2000" and are amused at the skull-and-crossbones emblems on all the signs. You assume all the DANGER warnings are there to make the run appear more thrilling. But no sooner have you pushed off and you realize two important things: (1) There's not a slope here—all you see are trees, boulders, and cliffs; and (2) You really could have used some more instruction about how to maneuver and stop. The next day you have plenty of time to consider what Baltasar Gracian wisely said, "To know very little and yet seek the ambitious path is to court ruin." It's all you can think about as you gaze out your hospital window.

Few of us would be foolish enough to commit too soon to something that could harm us physically. Yet it's all too common to see people who know very little get too ambitious with their jobs, key relationships, or financial nest eggs. They frequently discover that aggressive and risky behavior can indeed be a "path to ruin." They find out, too late, that the slope is too steep.

Note carefully that this doesn't mean we must always avoid the more challenging paths. We simply need to learn what we're doing first. Running the Class IV rapids may be a goal at some point in your future. You just need to make sure your rafting skills first include more than drifting down a lazy river on an inner tube.

Better safe than sorry, they say. Yet the better you get at what you enjoy, the more opportunities you can take advantage of, and the less sorry you will be.

SAY NO TO NOTORIETY

Avoid being notorious in everything. Being notorious can develop from being unusual. That person will be a loner. Even beauty can be discredited by excess, because it offends others by the extreme notice it attracts. Even in intellectual pursuits, a lack of moderation may produce empty discussions.

The concept of being "notorious" has been somewhat romanticized in our culture. We see notorious people on *America's Most Wanted.* Their photos hang on the post office walls, courtesy of the FBI. But we need to be clear about the designation. If we're not careful, the concept of being notorious is equated with being popular, sought after, or desired.

Many of us have an inner desire to be perceived as notorious. We want a reputation for being eccentric and on the edge. But we don't actually think through the consequences. When someone says, "He's a notorious ladies' man," the person in question might take pride in the reputation he has developed. But all it means is that women are being warned to stay away from him! A notorious gambler is not someone you want to attend Casino Night at your child's school. A notorious driver is not someone you want to carpool with. And if you're throwing a dinner party for family and friends, the people on those wanted posters are actually the least wanted people at your table.

Even in areas such as beauty and academics, a notorious reputation is one that tends to repel rather than attract others. Perhaps you've been stuck trying to talk to a professor or scientist whose interests lie in only one area. You can't keep up with him, and you soon discover that he's so devoted to his work that he's never seen an episode of *Cheers*, never been to the beach, and isn't aware of any music that's been released since the Carpenters. It is difficult to accept or converse with such a person.

Do we really want a reputation for being notorious, or would we prefer a reputation for being approachable, likable, fun loving, fascinating? One choice and you find yourself in for a lonely lifestyle. The other, and you'll soon be among the most desired in your community.

BECAUSE I SAID SO!

Be trustworthy. Honorable dealing with others is no longer common. Few people keep their word. Whole nations break promises and are deceitful. This bad behavior should be a warning rather than an example. A person of honor should never forget who he is just because others are different.

Have you ever noticed how many "legends" about famous people have to do with their honesty? We hear of George Washington confessing to chopping down the cherry tree. We hear of Abraham Lincoln walking for miles to repay a debt of a few cents. And while some people question the authenticity of some of these stories, they miss the point. Whether true or not, the motives of trustworthiness, honesty, and honor are the stuff of legends.

Most of us need little prodding from others to know we should keep our promises and be honest with others. We know it is the right thing to be truthful, even when we don't practice it. Yet we may unintentionally ignore one important area of keeping promises. And a more recent president set a good example for us.

George Bush piloted a plane that was shot down during World War II. He was forced to parachute to safety. At that time, he made a promise to himself that some day he would make a parachute jump just for fun and not because he had to. As his political career took him to the White House and beyond, his promise to himself went unfulfilled. But as a retired former president, he finally went out at seventy-two years of age and made his first planned jump.

How many things do we promise ourselves that we never get around to doing? We all aspire to hopes and dreams that may not be reached, yet there are other attainable goals we want to (and could) achieve if we would commit to the time and energy required. If we don't even keep these promises to ourselves, how can we be trustworthy in regard to others?

They say charity begins at home. Honesty begins even closer. If it's not within you to begin with, it's never going to flow outward to others. Do everyone a favor. Sometime this week, keep a promise you've made to yourself—not because somebody else says so but because *you* did.

THE MAN BEHIND THE CURTAIN

Make use of your absence to make yourself more valued. Someone who is regarded as a lion in his absence may be laughed at when present. It is easier to see the exterior shell than the kernel of greatness it encloses. Imagination is larger than sight and affects the opinion of you in public.

In *The Wizard of Oz,* the residents of the Emerald City are scared silly of "the great and powerful wizard" who occasionally appears amid smoke and thunder. Near the end of the film, Toto pulls back a curtain to reveal that the wizard is actually a man—a quite ordinary man, at that.

Most of us have had similar revelations about people who didn't meet our original expectations. Perhaps it was seeing a disc jockey for the first time and realizing the scrawny, bald man didn't live up to the rich and full voice you loved so much. Or maybe you are impressed with an actor's performance and then see the real person on a talk show—shallow, self-centered, and not all that bright. When it comes to some people, the better you get to know them, the less you begin to like them.

If we're smart, we don't give others the opportunity to foster similar opinions about us. We need not be ashamed of who we are or intentionally deceive anyone, yet we need to be aware that many people will look for any chink in our armor where they might take advantage of us.

Let's not forget that after Dorothy met the man who had presumed to be the Wizard of Oz, he turned out to be quite helpful to her and her friends. He wasn't the god-like figure they had thought, but neither was he an evil person. Perhaps we need to come to the same conclusions about others or ourselves.

Of course, Dorothy's wizard turned out to be a dream. In contrast, we must face the harsh realities of life as we present an image to others. Learn to let your "kernel of greatness" come through in creative ways. And remember that even though you aren't a wizard, you can still use a disappearing act more frequently and let your absence work to your advantage.

RESPONSIBLE TO A POINT

Do not try to be responsible for all people, otherwise you become a slave. Freedom is more precious than any gift for which you may be tempted to give it up. Put more focus on staying independent and less on making others dependent on you. The sole advantage of power is that you can do more good for others.

It's a good feeling to be needed, at least at first. When parents begin to age, it's an honor to have the opportunity to care for them as they cared for you. When people at work have problems to share, your wisdom comes shining through, and they come to count on your opinion and/or involvement. It's hard to say no when your church sends out the call for volunteers to work with hungry and homeless people. If a spouse or child becomes seriously ill, they count on you being there for them. And if these events pile up, the feeling of warmth and concern you originally felt can quickly evolve into one of fatigue, dread, and hopelessness. Slavery.

Of course you want to take care of your close family, so you need to be careful about committing to other responsibilities. If you want to help anyone, you need a healthy body and objective mind. You may be able to do more for your parents by taking care of yourself and being there during emergencies rather than draining your own health by trying to spend every spare minute with them. You might do more for the homeless by providing financial support rather than volunteer work. Everyone's situation is different, so it's up to you to determine what is best in your case.

The goal is not to stop helping people. Rather, we need to learn to help others without losing our independence. We want to help them based on our schedules and priorities, not theirs. We can't always determine the most convenient times or limit our involvement to the extent we wish, but sometimes we can. Whenever possible, we need to value and protect our freedom.

Only after we learn to help others because we want to rather than because we feel obligated to, do we discover what helping people is really all about.

A PASSION FOR PEACE

Never act out of passion. If you are not behaving normally, you can't act in your own best interest. Find a calm mediator who acts as a go-between to keep you cool. As soon as you see that you are losing your temper, beat a wise retreat because when the blood is up it is soon spilled.

We can't help feeling passionate about certain things. Emotions are part of life, and sometimes those emotions become quite strong. Love, lust, anger, jealousy, hatred—any of these emotions, good or bad, can become passions.

We can, however, keep from acting based on the passionate feelings within us. We need to respond to emotions but not allow them to control us. Passionate feelings can quickly lead to passionate actions. And as soon as we let passion control our actions, it becomes impossible to backtrack.

Think of actions in the past that you desperately wish you could take back yet cannot. A slap. A humiliating and abusive insult. A look of hatred. Deserting someone during a time of need. As hard as you try to convince the person that you really didn't mean it, your action (or inaction) has spoken much louder than your words.

At the very least, we must learn to put some time and distance between our passions and our actions. Many times that's all it takes to let blood pressure come down and hot heads cool off. Once calm, we can make an intelligent response to whatever it was that threatened to set us off.

If time doesn't diminish the heat, however, the next step is to put another person between our passions and our actions. If we are correct in our assessment of the situation, an objective third party will confirm it. If not, however, we're more likely to listen to the mediator than the person we feel so passionately about.

When you're cooking on a grill, sometimes the fire gets too hot to cook properly. You need to throw some water on it to let off steam and keep the heat at a manageable level. The coals continue to burn hot, but at a slightly lower intensity, the heat serves a beneficial purpose.

Don't lose your passions. Just don't lose control of them and end up getting burned.

A PARTY WAITING TO HAPPEN

Let your personal qualities surpass the requirements of your role in life. Do not let it be the other way around. Your extensive abilities should expand as you climb higher in your responsibilities. On the other hand, narrow-minded people will lose heart as their reputation diminishes. Your own confidence will find true opportunity.

"That's not in my job description!"

In work settings, some people get testy if you ask them to do anything they don't feel is their responsibility. Yet in refusing to do anything beyond what is printed on a sheet of paper, they voluntarily diminish their personal qualities. That's not a good idea.

Job descriptions are important in that they lay out certain tasks by which we will be evaluated once a year or so. We need to meet and exceed those expectations. But people evaluate us by our personal qualities every single day. You've probably passed judgment on those who moved up a corporate ladder and seemed to lose more vestiges of personality the higher they got. Don't let others say the same about you.

The more responsibility and influence we have, the more important it is to let noble human qualities shine through. Any task becomes unbearably bleak when deprived of the elements of humanness: humor, sharing, empathy, sincerity, and so forth. We need to worry more about our life descriptions than our job descriptions.

Of course, we'll occasionally run into bosses and coworkers who tend to take advantage when we choose to be willing servants. But in such cases, it is always better to deal with the problem from a personal standpoint ("I think you're taking advantage of my good nature.") than to immediately let a job description speak for us.

People are like balloons. We're pretty dull in our basic deflated state. At the other extreme, we can take on too much and get stretched so thin that we're in danger of exploding. But when we find the right balance and acquire an appropriate fullness, we carry a party atmosphere with us wherever we go.

THE PURSUIT OF HAPPINESS

When all is said and done, be a saint. Three things make a person happy: health, holiness, and wisdom. A person's capacity and greatness are measured by his virtue and not by his fortune. Virtue alone is sufficient. She makes people lovable in life and memorable after death.

If you were asked to list the things that would make you happy, what would be on your Top-Three list? To be honest, few of us might have health, holiness, and wisdom on the top of our lists, yet what more do we need?

Health allows us to work hard, to care for others, to have high energy, to be in good physical shape, and to enjoy life more. Holiness keeps us in touch with God and gives us a more meaningful perspective on life with higher purposes and goals. Wisdom allows us to make good choices, to offer helpful advice to those who need it, and to know when to say yes and when to say no. With these three basics, we can accomplish almost anything we desire. Could we say the same if the list included lots of cash? A doctorate? A better job? A home in a better climate?

Everyone wants success and peace of mind. The trouble is, many of us try to surround ourselves with external things, hoping inner peace will somehow be absorbed. If we begin with the right internal qualities, contentment will flow outward. That's a sure formula for success.

Are there limits to how healthy, holy, and wise we should attempt to be? Well, sainthood makes a nice goal. Otherwise it's too easy to plateau and think, "Well, I'm a good enough person now. I'll stop trying so hard to be nice." When wisdom and holiness are genuine, the path to maturity and success is a lifelong one. Besides, when it comes to headgear, most people look much more attractive in a halo than a dunce cap.

HANDLE WITH CARESS

Do not be made of glass in your relationships. Some people break easily and show a lack of consistency. They have to be treated with great delicacy and sensitivity. They are egotistical and moody. But the one who truly loves is diamond-like: hard and everlasting.

What's wrong with glass? Many respected people and places are famous because of their association with glassmaking: Tiffany, Wedgwood, Fabergé, Waterford, Limoges. Some of the most beautiful artifacts in the world are made of glass. Shouldn't our relationships be just as beautiful?

There's nothing wrong with beauty in a friendship, but even more important is durability. The very delicacy that makes glass so beautiful can quickly destroy a relationship. One slight jostle can chip fine glass and reduce its value drastically. A significant jolt can shatter it, rendering it worthless. That's not what we should look for in friendships.

Life is filled with unexpected storms, quakes, shipwrecks, and worse. We want to seek out people who will endure the roughest of times with us. We don't want friends who crack at the first little tremble. Nor do we want to be such friends.

The place for glass is on a shelf, protected and secure. But trying to live life on a shelf is as dull as it gets. A full life will include some white-water rapids, some harsh jolts, many rough patches, and several leaps of faith. It's no place for glass.

We should not expect people to always handle us with care. Sometimes it's enough to realize that they're just keeping in touch. So hold on tightly to those you love as you go through life and enjoy the ride.

THE LONG ROUTE TO POPULARITY

Have nothing to do with disreputable pursuits. Avoid fads that bring you less than a good reputation. There are people with bizarre tastes that take to heart everything the wise reject. They love the eccentric. Though they are well known they are eventually ridiculed.

It's not hard to make a reputation for yourself. All you have to do is be willing to be more outrageous than anyone else. Drink harder. Swear more profusely. Go streaking in public places where no on else dares. Eat vile and disgusting things to the amusement of others. You'll get a reputation in no time. The trouble is, it's a less-than-good one.

A reputation made quickly for audacious behavior does not easily disappear. Howard Stern rose to the top in shock radio but speaks with great disappointment now that some people don't want to consider him a "serious actor." Bill Clinton smoked marijuana back when everyone was doing it. Later, as president of the United States, he didn't have much success at trying to downplay his involvement when he said he did not inhale.

There are no shortcuts to maturity. We all want to be popular and well liked. Yet if we want the respect of others as mature adults, it must begin when we are younger. We must be careful to avoid disreputable pursuits—no matter how well they seem to work as attention getters and reputation makers.

The day may come when someone looks to you for leadership. Others, of course, will oppose you. Why make it easy for your opponents to pull out photos of your previous actions, quite embarrassing in light of the mature qualities you are now trying to display? How much better to let them look in vain for anything you might be ashamed of.

Let others pursue "bizarre tastes" to get attention. Let tawdry fads come and go. In the long run, the person who has avoided all such things will be the one who stands out in a crowd.

RUNNING A HIGH TEMPERAMENT

A bad temperament spoils everything—even reason and justice. A good one aids everything, even sweetens truth and adds beauty to old age itself. Fine behavior steals people's hearts and a pleasant expression can help you out of difficult situations in unusual ways.

Think back to high school when you were signing up for classes. Can you recall wishing, hoping, begging to get a certain teacher for a difficult course? To be more truthful, you were hoping to avoid one teacher in particular. In many cases, this teacher had a reputation for being the best in his or her field, yet the temperament of the person made students duck and cover at the mention of his or her name.

Temperament makes more of a difference in relationships than many people realize. It doesn't matter how wonderful a person is after you get to know him, if his bad temperament doesn't attract others in the first place. You can be filled with "reason and justice," but if a job interviewer only sees what is perceived as a bad attitude, you aren't likely to get the job. On the other hand, a good temperament works to a person's advantage, even when the person is something of a scamp. While you're thinking about high school, see if you can't remember several mischief-makers who never seemed to get into serious trouble because of charm that allowed them to talk their way out of punishment. We need to learn from such people—not how to escape justice but rather how to use temperament to our advantage.

The story is told of a country guy who sent all his city friends a country ham for Christmas. When he later asked each person how they liked them, they sheepishly explained that the ham had arrived moldy, so they threw it out. Country ham, you may know, frequently develops a thin layer of mold in storage, but you wipe it off to get to some of the best tasting meat available.

We should never let a "moldy" temperament prevent us from seeing the value of other people. And when it's up to us, we need to clean up our temperaments so others don't reject us prematurely. We get concerned when our temperature gets too far from normal. Are we just as aware of fluctuations in temperament? If not, perhaps it's time for a checkup.

AN UPSTREAM BATTLE

Never take things against the grain, no matter how they may come. Everything has both a smooth and a rough side. The best weapon wounds if received by the blade rather than the staff. Many things cause pain that would cause pleasure if you saw their advantages, so look to the better side.

Suppose friends invite you to go whitewater rafting and you eagerly accept. But when you get there, you discover they have arranged to run the course backward, beginning downriver and trying to paddle upstream all the way. The exhilaration you expected to feel is soon replaced by frustration, sore muscles, and rude comments from rafters trying to navigate the traditional way.

Or suppose you attend an exhibition between two skilled swordsmen who decide to hold their weapons by the blades and attempt to strike one another with the hilts. Instead of a demonstration of skill and agility, you're likely to witness a comic display reminiscent of the Three Stooges.

It's ludicrous to think of scenes such as these. People simply wouldn't be so foolish. Yet in real life we may attempt similarly silly endeavors by going against the flow to the extreme. Good woodworkers and painters know the importance of going with the grain. Why don't accountants, sales people, CEOs, middle managers, and other workers?

Sometimes we have the choice of taking the easy way or the hard way. Why waste energy doing things the hard way when, by cooperating, we could accomplish much more with the same energy?

No one would argue that there will be times when we must go against the flow because of principle or virtue. Yet to fight the mainstream simply to be different is frequently a waste of time and effort. We know well the story of the salmon that swim upstream, fighting desperately to go against the raging currents. But they have a good reason: When they get there, they spawn and begin another life cycle for their species. If you plan to go to the same trouble, you first need to ask, "What's in this for me?" Otherwise, you just look like a fish out of water.

PASSING THE BUCK

Do pleasant things yourself, but do unpleasant things through others. By the first approach you gain goodwill, by the second you avoid hatred. In a high position you can only work through rewards and punishment, so give the first yourself, and inflict the second through your subordinates.

You might suspect that we are advocating a cold-hearted approach to management. Yet now, most corporations are set up according to this philosophy. When a boss wants to do an "unpleasant thing" such as fire someone, he or she probably has a personnel department (or at least a person) to do it for him. If a person needs to be demoted, the news usually comes through a middle manager rather than the CEO.

We also need to consider that the context of his statement is not one of close personal relationships. Think of a board member of a Fortune 500 company or a military general who has thousands of people under his authority yet doesn't know many of them by name. For the good of the company or group, the person at the top needs to be perceived as a benevolent and capable leader. If he or she personally came around to deliver bad news to individuals, the person's approach would always carry with it a sense of dread. That's where the wise use of subordinates can cushion the blows.

Of course, when dealing with those close to you, the announcement of bad news comes easier from your lips than from some underling. No one can avoid all unpleasant things, no matter how much money and power he has or how many people he or she controls. A street-smart leader knows when to shoulder the burden herself and when to delegate to others.

Passing the buck has almost purely negative connotations in our society. However, it is occasion-ally prudent to hand off unpleasant duties to someone else. Yet perhaps you can redefine passing the buck as handing out raises and bonuses. If and when you prove yourself a leader who delights in the joys of rewarding others, you'll be more quickly forgiven for less joyous decisions.

SAVING FOR A SUNNY DAY

Live for the moment. Act when you can, for time and tide wait for no one. Do not live by fixed rules, except those that relate to the virtues. You may have to drink the water tomorrow that you throw out today. The polestar of prudence is steered by the prevailing wind.

Have you ever received a gift certificate for your favorite restaurant and decided to use it for a special occasion? Yet perhaps on your birthday you weren't feeling well and on your anniversary you had other plans, so the certificate expired without your benefiting from it. We all let good opportunities pass us by because we're waiting for a better time. We learn the hard way that sometimes there is no better time than now.

Complete this sentence: "Someday I'll get around to _____." If you're like most people, several things come to mind immediately. We all have hopes and plans. We're waiting for just the right time to do them. As important as these things are to us, we tend to wait for a convenient time rather than acting when we can and getting the job done.

Sometimes the problem is we've been cautioned strongly not to attempt too much. We're warned to save for a rainy day and not put all our eggs in one basket. Frugality and planning for the future are certainly important, yet we need to make sure that fear does not prevent action. We must find a balance between acting now and saving for tomorrow.

Perhaps you hear the voices of parents or others in your mind, warning you, "Don't go overboard!" It's good advice. If we get too ambitious as we sail through life, we risk getting tossed right over the rail. But it's just as bad to go under-board. If you stay below and never get out on deck, your outlook on life is going to be quite bleak indeed.

COMPLETELY BAKED

Never let things be seen half finished. They can only be enjoyed when complete. All beginnings are misshapen, and the deformity sticks in our minds. Take a lesson from the Creator, who never brings the child to light until it is fit to be seen.

When you order an omelet in a restaurant, there's a good reason the chef doesn't bring it to your table when it's half done to see what you think about it. When it's finished, it sits on your plate looking light, fluffy, and appetizing. But halfway through the process, you would see the swirling grease in the pan, the runny and gooey egg, and possibly some other things that are best left to the eyes of the kitchen crew.

The lesson for us is to make sure we don't pitch our ideas and suggestions until they're suitable for consideration. We may see the anticipated finished result clearly in our own minds, yet another person's imagination may not be nearly as vivid.

A good advertising agency doesn't simply talk the client through a proposed ad. They will use storyboards and other aids to present it in an almost-finished form. A salesperson feels much more confident if he or she can use a prototype of the product while making the sales pitch. The potential customer feels much more assured to see something that looks like a product rather than something that merely sounds like one.

In *The Graduate,* Ben (the protagonist) is accused of having an idea that is half baked. His reply is, "No, it's not. It's completely baked." It was a humorous line in Buck Henry's screenplay. Yet it reflects an important truth. May we ensure that our own ideas are always fully baked and ready to be served to others for their nourishment.

HAND-Y ADVICE

Never entrust your confidence to someone else unless you have his pledge as well. If honor is at stake, act with a partner, so that each of you will be careful of the other's honor. Let the danger be in common and the risk mutual.

Wouldn't it be nice if someone would invent a device to ensure that a partner had to take all the same risks in life that you do, that he or she would have to face all the same trials and challenges you must endure? Actually, such a device already exists and is quite affordable. All you need to do is buy a set of handcuffs and chain yourself to the other person. What you do, he does as well. And vice versa. All risks and rewards are equally shared.

You've seen this tactic numerous times in movies and on TV. It's how a detective makes sure a shifty criminal doesn't sneak away. It's how a frustrated person gets someone else's attention. With handcuffs, the other person is always within arm's reach.

The trouble is, we may want to share confidences and risks with more than one person. It's difficult enough for two people to maneuver while wearing handcuffs, much less three or more. So we need a more practical way of dealing with others.

While physical ties may be impractical, we can still be clear about our expectations in terms of shared emotional or moral responsibilities. If a sibling doesn't want to send an aging parent to a nursing home, it might be wise to ensure that he sees what it's like to do home care. If a business partner wants to risk your cash reserves and reputation on a questionable venture, make sure she risks her own first. Many people like to gamble when it's "on the house." Therefore, we need to make sure we do not become "the house" for the risk-taking pursuits of others.

When you deal with people of honor, however, you don't need to take such precautions. They won't expect more of you than they do of themselves. They volunteer to share danger and risk. You won't need handcuffs in such instances. A handshake will do just fine.

CHAPTER AND VERSATILITY

Become a versatile person. A person of many excellent qualities equals the worth of many people. Variety in excellence is the delight of life. Impart the full scope of your enjoyment of life to your circle of friends and followers, and thereby enrich their lives.

One of the most popular TV shows of the 1980s was *MacGyver*. The title character was a model of versatility. His creative mind could solve any problem. Nuclear plant going into meltdown? Fix it with a tennis racket. Imprisoned on a remote island? Make an airplane out of a lawnmower engine, an exhaust fan, and some old sheets. Even his ever-present Swiss army knife symbolized his vast versatility.

You've also seen portrayals of the other extreme— nuclear scientists who were incapable of replacing a fuse at home, or renowned artists who couldn't drive or balance a checkbook. Perhaps some people overreact when they hear the description, jack-of-all-trades, master of none. While it's good to be extremely knowledgeable in one specific area, we also need to develop "variety in excellence." We need depth of knowledge in our chosen fields, yet we also need breadth of knowledge in real life.

It's not too tough to develop versatility. It can be quite fun, actually. Watch *Jeopardy*. Play trivia games with friends. Read books (or at least magazines) about interesting topics you know little about. Watch a PBS special instead of a rerun of your favorite sitcom (or vice versa). Take an adult-education class. Listen to a different radio station once in a while.

You might be surprised at how quickly your newfound versatility will make a difference. You'll find yourself understanding references that previously made no sense. You'll be able to take part in more conversations. With enough practice, you may even start to understand some of the things your kids talk about!

The longest books are absorbed a chapter at a time. The same regular commitment to versatility will soon allow you to equal the worth of many and enrich the lives of those around you. You may never be the next MacGyver, but at least you can learn how to change a fuse.

ABOUT THE AUTHORS

James S. Bell Jr., the Editorial Director of Moody Press, is a leading authority on Christian devotional classics. He has updated such works as *Beautiful Living* by James R. Miller and *In His Steps* by Charles Sheldon, both published by Honor Books. His goal is to bring the great writings from the past into the hearts and lives of a new generation of readers.

Stan Campbell has been a full-time writer for the last ten years. He has authored and co-authored several books including *The Complete Idiots Guide to the Bible,* which he co-authored with James S. Bell Jr.

Additional copies of this book
are available from your local bookstore.

If you have enjoyed this book, or if it has
impacted your life, we would like to hear from you.
Please contact us at:
RiverOak Publishing
Department E
P.O. Box 700143
Tulsa, Oklahoma 74170-0143